CREATING YOUR PERSONAL JOURNEY

D1510742

CREATING YOUR PERSONAL JOURNEY

A Primer: To Discover Who You Are
And To Uncover Your True Desires

By

Roger L. Paradis

CONCORD PRESS,
CONCORD, MASSACHUSETTS

Concord Press
60 Thoreau St., #236
Concord, MA 01742-9116

Copyright © 1995 by Roger L. Paradis

First Printing 1995

Publisher's Cataloging in Publication Data
Paradis, Roger L.

Creating Your Personal Journey, A Primer: To Discover
Who You Are And To Uncover Your True Desires By
Roger L. Paradis

1. Conduct of Life
2. Individuality
3. Life skills

ISBN 0-9643604-0-3(Softcover)
Library of Congress Catalog Card Number: 94-069155

Printed in the United States of America

TABLE OF CONTENTS

FORWARD

It is time for us as a society and as individuals to begin again. In the late 1700s, we won our fight for freedom as a country. Now each of us may start again to become personally free.

To become personally free, the freedom we gain must come from within. We must learn to raise our awareness and discover who we are, and what we want to do and be.

Too often we work for a lifetime in hopes that we can have a few years of retirement in which to do what we really want to do and to be what we really want to be. For most of us, discovering who we are is a twenty, thirty, or forty year activity of trial and error. We have few guidelines to help us reach the answer. We try one line of work, and if that does not satisfy, we try a new career. Too often, we run out of years before we find an answer.

I have gone through the same trial and error, but I do think I have found my answer. My period of discovery started in 1963, the year I graduated from college. My period of trial and error, with many trials and several errors, ended in 1990. The answer to who I am and what I want to do came in my writing. The answers to the many questions I had came very rapidly after I began to write this book.

During my period of analysis, I realized that every project on which I had worked resulted in my writing a book, manual, or pamphlet. My writing skills were trying to manifest themselves as a part of my destiny -- my journey. Now as I become more consciously aware of these writing skills, they are becoming a greater part of my focus.

We all need to become aware of our primary area of focus. We all have a journey to make. As we clear our system of hate, doubt, myths, and fear, our journey becomes clearer and brighter. As we come to know ourselves, these negative attributes give way to love, faith, truth, wisdom and courage. Our distractions are diminished. We become better attuned to the natural laws, and, as a result, well-being and joy enter our lives.

CHAPTER 1

INTRODUCTION

Everyone has the power within to shape and control his/her own life. Everyone has the power to create his/her personal journey. What decisions we make and what roads we take are dependent on the quality of our thoughts and actions.

By raising our awareness 12 ways, we raise the quality of our thoughts and actions. Our self-image and self-esteem improve with the quality of our thoughts and actions. With a good self-image and high self-esteem, we clear away many of the negative blockages in our minds and redirect our communications in a positive way.

Quality has become one of the dominant themes in our society. People are searching for something better. For some, this translates into more and better products and a bigger, better home. Accumulation of property and products is the primary thrust. Security is provided by having as much as possible. Gradually, however, we become aware that accumulation, while somewhat satisfying, has only a temporary effect on the quality of our lives. It does satisfy our basest need for survival and security. It does provide a degree of happiness. But it does not provide the well-being and the joy that we desire. Usually after enjoying the new product for a period of time, we are compelled to buy another product that will bring some temporary satisfaction.

In our society we judge success by what people have. We base our happiness on what products and property we can obtain. When we purchase an automobile, for instance, we feel great pride and happiness. As the automobile ages, our degree of happiness declines. Well-being and joy in our lives cannot be provided by only the things we have. And, so, many begin again to search for tangible and intangible ways to add substance to their lives.

CREATING YOUR PERSONAL JOURNEY

To bring deeper, lasting meaning to our lives, we must answer two questions -- Who are we? What do we do?

We can get closer to the answer to those two questions by raising our awareness in any of the twelve ways. We must uncover who we are by peeling away the layers of myths, guilts, and phobias that have covered our true identity, an identity formed by absorbing poor advice and misinformation. We must clear away the negative blockages that have been placed in the pathways of our mind.

Many people never ask themselves the above two questions. They are what others want them to be and they do what it takes to survive the rigors of their daily lives. They believe that first they will work hard and accumulate everything that they need. They prepare a plan for their financial security that will take them to the end of their lives. The logic is that, once they've worked hard enough, they will have everything that they need and then will have time to be what they want to be and do what they want to do. The journey to obtain what they have is often a tortuous journey through years of work, in exchange for a few years of happiness in retirement. Too often we believe our financial plan is a guide for more than financial security. We believe that it is an end in itself, that it will bring well-being and joy. Rather than following a plan, most people use trial and error to discover who they are and what they do. It usually takes twenty or thirty years to reach the right answer.

But life is much more joyful if the two questions are answered prior to the period of accumulation. Once they are answered, the things really worth having flow from what we want to be and what we want to do. The choices become more logical. The things we have create harmony in our lives rather than being appendages.

To answer the question of who we are, we must look within ourselves and consider the physical, the intellectual, and the spiritual. To answer the question of what we do, we must consider our actions, and evaluate the quality they add to our lives.

We are all provided with a unique purpose in our lives. We all have a destiny. We can only fulfill that purpose and complete that destiny if we uncover and understand who we are. We are all here to love and to be loved. We are all here to love and to contribute to others. We can only love if we operate from a positive mindset, free of fears and anger

2

and hate. Fear and anger and hate are created by being something other than who we are.

Almost everyone's goal is "feeling great". We study or work all week hoping that on weekends we can translate all that hard work into a few hours of great happiness. But happiness is so elusive. If we are successful in one area of our lives, another unattended area seems to fall apart. How can we keep our lives balanced?

There is one thing we can always count on -- the resoluteness of the human spirit that springs from within us. And because we are so resolute, we are able to bounce back, time and time again, from let-downs and disappointments. When we pause in our activity and when we think, or when we go to sleep with a certain peace, we invariably find a new direction and a new solution to our problems. Optimism, hope, and faith continually spring up within us and give us new purpose.

We awake from a peaceful meditation and we feel good again. We want that feeling to continue. But what is that feeling? It is total confidence. Everything seems to be in harmony. We see clearly, and solutions appear easy. Resting has given us a fresh perspective. Then we usually make a very crucial mistake. We go charging out to do as much as we can do to preserve that confident feeling. We work harder. We exercise more. We try to eat the proper foods. We are determined to avoid the pitfalls and not to repeat the mistakes that got us into the last mess. But then we start losing our energy, and begin to operate with less brain power. The feeling, which led to a great surge of action, begins to dissipate. The energy and the feeling dissipate because we forget to look internally.

We begin to operate externally, only, in exchanges with others. To keep our lives balanced and to maintain a constant source of energy, we must learn to use our complete communication path. There are two parts to that path, the internal part and the external part.

The process starts by learning to rely on our intuition. We can find many examples of the times our intuition has provided us with the answers we needed. We do not see our intuitive answers as coming from a logical extension of our mind. We consider our intuition as some mysterious energy that sporadically provides some good advice. Most of us, however, have said many times, "I should have followed my intuition." Start with a simple little test. The next time you get an idea and you feel really refreshed and you start to charge out the door, STOP! Go back to your chair, sit down, and ask yourself: Where did the idea come from? You will find it did not come from another person. You were the creator of that idea. If we are smart enough to create these ideas, why can't we be smart enough to generate a total plan of action?

Go beyond the idea itself. Ask yourself what the next step should be. When you get the next step, ask yourself for another step until it all unfolds clearly. There is no need to discuss this with others. The answers will continue to come to you from your intuition. We all have the ability within us to simplify our lives and to enjoy them to their fullest.

Why does this all work? All the great masters and teachers have explained it, repeating the same advice. Look within for the answers. The solutions are not outside ourselves. What does this advice mean? It means that we all have a direct line to the Supreme Being. When we reach maturity, we do not need any external intermediaries. When we train our intuition with daily practice, we cultivate that direct line and it becomes more powerful. We ask and we receive.

Our primary connection is from the conscious mind to our subconscious mind and to the universal energy. The universal energy flows within us and all around us. All the answers can flow from within our subconscious to our conscious and surface as answers from our intuition.

When our primary connection becomes other human beings, all the answers we get are diluted by the perceptions and understandings of others. Each one of us is unique. We must develop a way to consciously think of our innermost desires and present them inwardly to our subconscious mind rather than to the outside world. It is the most reliable way to achieve results.

To learn to do this effectively, we must begin again. During our initial journey from birth through our teens to adulthood, many decisions were made for us, forcing us to select certain paths. Our will was not free. But at some point in our lives, we are all free to place our future growth in our own hands. That point in our lives is difficult for all of us. But we all recognize that time when it arrives. It comes at a time when we just know we have reached a maturity that says,

4

INTRODUCTION

"I am going to take charge of my life and I am going to contribute to someone or something."

When we reach maturity, we are free to be. We can be who we are. But first we must clear away the mask that has been formed by perceptions, beliefs, and truths of others. Og Mandino in his book, The Greatest Miracle in the World, in a chapter titled "The God Memorandum," said it well when he said, "This is your birthday. This is your new date of birth. Your first life, like unto a play at the theatre, was only a rehearsal. This time the curtain is up. This time the world watches and waits to applaud. This time you will not fail."[1]

We must forget all the beliefs we hold, unless they meet the inner test. There is no complete set of beliefs and truths outside ourselves that can define who we are or determine what we should do. Knowledge and truth are within us, if we listen to our intuition.

One very good example of the use of intuition appeared in a Boston Globe article on April 23, 1990, written by Frank Mauran. R. Doolittle had a nine-year old son, Simon, who played in Little League. Simon was having great difficulty hitting the baseball. Bob prayed for a solution. Then, while he was praying, an idea "dropped into his head." He took an old ski pole and fastened it to a whiffle ball with about two feet of telephone wire. While Bob held the pole, Simon hit the ball. The Hitmaster was born. Simon became a good hitter and eventually made the All-Star team. Bob had turned inward for a solution. His solution turned into a family business. At the time of the article, Bob had sold over 1,000 Hitmasters.

If, as an adult, we choose to start again and to be who we are, we can transcend the limitations of our heritage and our environment. How many of us start again? Not many. But we have all heard about people who profess to have been born again. Usually driven by some crises, they reevaluate their lives. They discover that they have put too much emphasis on one part of their lives, and so they readjust. In most cases, the drive is away from what they have to a more personal, spiritual life. Generally, when people are in a crisis, they are unable to act. All of their friends seem to desert them. All avenues of escape and access to power are blocked. The more they do, the more they seem to sink into a quagmire.

It's at that point, when people cease to fight, that the transition usually occurs and they let go. They let the flow

CREATING YOUR PERSONAL JOURNEY

take them. Whereas they had been struggling against the current, trying to swim through the rapids, they now float, their energy sapped. At that point people discover, to their amazement, that the worst has happened. They have cut themselves off from everything external, including their friends, their fellow workers, and their relatives. But somehow, they are more at peace. They reject the view that they are bad people. They admit that perhaps they have made some mistakes. They realize that their priorities have created an imbalance in their lives. At that point, they reach inward. They begin to question every belief and truth they hold. The results are usually outstanding. Because they have discarded everything in their lives that caused them trouble, their minds are clear and they are at peace. Now they are free to let the inner knowledge and truth flow in. Their old beliefs and "truths" that got them into so much trouble start to crumble. The blockages they created are removed. They are beginning.

Think back on your own experiences. Think back to the people you have known publicly and personally who have had similar experiences. If you have the opportunity, ask them how they made the transition that changed their lives.

How can each of us start again? How can each of us change and improve the building blocks that form us?

Let us start by becoming more familiar with twelve of those building blocks. At any stage in our lives, the quality of the building blocks or components determines the quality of our lives. Each building block can be shaped by our thoughts, by our actions, and by what we have. How can we improve each building block to find fulfillment? We start by looking inside. We evaluate every part of our lives. We ask ourselves how we got to where we are. We review the decisions that were made. We question every belief and truth we hold. Then we wait patiently for the answers through our direct line.

INTRODUCTION

The twelve components or building blocks that we must review and evaluate are:

Nutrition	Material Possessions
Exercise	Biology
Work	Environment
Play	Freedom
Rest	Spirituality
Education	Contribution

Why do these components shape us? Every thought and every action in our lives contributes to who we are and to what we do. The reciprocal is also true--who we are and what we do determines our thoughts and our actions. We can think or do only to the extent that we are aware. Our awareness limits our perceptions and our beliefs to only those of which we are aware. To increase, change, or improve our awareness, we must become aware of other thoughts, beliefs, or truths. Our self-image is a composite of all that we are aware of in the twelve components. If we improve or change positively our awareness in any component, we improve our self-image.

Our self-image is contained in our subconscious. Our subconscious contains the sum total of every thought we have had and every action we have taken. If we can change the content of our subconscious by becoming more aware of things of higher quality, we can raise our self-image, increase our confidence, and introduce more joy into our lives. If we think the earth is square, we have one set of beliefs. If we think the sun revolves around the earth, we have one set of beliefs. If we think the earth revolves around the sun, we have a different set of beliefs. Each set of beliefs, thoughts, and actions defines our unique character and develops our unique self-image.

Now, let us develop a brief definition of each of the twelve components and see how each can shape our lives. The twelve are listed in the rough order of emphasis in our society.

Material Possessions: This is everything we have. Having is very important in our society because it is thought to provide security and happiness. Most people believe that having everything they need will allow them to do the things they want to do so they can afford to be what they want to be. Material can be a powerful force in our lives for creating, constructing, or contributing. We can make having shape our lives more effectively, however, if we learn to let the material goods we need flow naturally from our thoughts and experiences rather than from manipulation.

Work: We are a career-oriented society. Our ambition is to work as hard as we can to achieve success, which is most often measured by our income. Our success or failure at work reverberates through all other parts of our lives. Work is at the center, with life's schedule dictated by our work schedule. Company owners control the tools of production. Employees control the labor they provide. To shape our lives through work, we must apply several techniques that help us work effectively in a team environment. To achieve maximum success in the workplace of today we must aspire to control the tools of production.

Education: For children, education is the center of their lives. Their concentration and focus in their formal school years most often dictates the success of their career. Education leads to awareness, which leads to change, which leads to maturity, which leads to growth. To shape our lives after our formal school years, we must extend the educational cycle so that we continue to mature and grow. Our formal school years teach us to communicate with society. Courses taken in our adult years should address our specialized needs combined with our inner needs.

Play: When we are finished with our studies and with our work, we play. Play provides relief from the tasks we must perform. How much time we have available for play depends on how quickly we can finish those tasks. However, play is our most natural state. When we play, we are more loving and giving. During play we generate a better balance of chemicals and hormones. Play is a flirtation with the id, the instinctual subconscious part of our personality. Play is our most creative time. To stay alive in the fullest sense, we would play all of our lives.

Spirituality: This is the most difficult component to grasp and to measure. Yet it is the simplest to apply and the most powerful for growth and change. We can and must learn to harness the power of spirituality. We must learn how to turn inward and develop our intuition until it becomes a part of our daily routine. We must learn to clear our direct line of all blockages which inhibit its transmission. Spirituality is not about the hereafter. Spirituality is about our life now.

Spirituality is each of us helping to prepare the Kingdom of God now for our well-being and joy.

Freedom: This is more basic than eating and drinking. Any attempt to stifle freedom will, in time, lead to revolt. Each person's freedom can be limited only to the extent that it jeopardizes the safety, security, and freedom of others. But lasting freedom is more psychological than physical. Only an indivi-dual's minimal freedom can be guaranteed by government. Higher degrees of freedom can be achieved only by breaking biological and psychological bonds. Freedom grows from a higher awareness of the twelve components that form our composite. More can be done for our individual freedom by clearing false values, fears, and phobias than by all the laws of government.

Nutrition: The smallest living units in our bodies are the cells. It is in the cells that the nutrients we provide interact with the supply of oxygen, hormones, and DNA to produce energy. The quality of the nutrients, to a large degree, determines the affectivity of our cells in producing proteins and enzymes that provide the energy. The cumulative production of all cells determines with what degree of enthusiasm, energy, and wisdom we function.

Exercise: Whereas nutrition provides the nutrients, exercise increases the supply of oxygen to the cells. The increase in oxygen improves formation of protein in the cells and make for a healthier flow in our system. A good exercise program will increase muscle strength, provide flexibility, and increase cardiovascular endurance. Overcoming inertia is the most difficult part of any exercise program. The mind must be motivated to move the body to dislodge the matter that is clogging our cells and bloodstream.

Rest: In the past, rest was required because we were physically tired. Today, we need rest because we are both mentally and physically tired. Because so many of our tasks require analysis and communication we build anxiety and stress during the days. Our information-oriented society requires the use of mental skills. Stress is a result of our tired minds trying to operate at peak. To shape our lives through rest, we must introduce a regimen of relaxation that contain techniques for rest periods of twenty seconds, two minutes, twenty minutes, two hours, and eight hours.

Contribution: There are many people working as volunteers in charitable organizations to love and improve the lot of others. These people in return gain the love of others, not necessarily from those they have loved. They contribute love for love. Others contribute clothes, goods, or money. We usually receive more than we give. The greatest dynamic to study for the proper lesson in contribution is the parent-child relationship. Parents contribute with no promise of return, but only because of a flow of love to the child. Fear of limitation often leads to comparison and competition rather than to contribution. If a perception of abundance for all can be cultivated, the flow of love to neighbor can be as compelling as the flow of love to one's children.

Environment: In our early years, our major environmental influences is our parents. Parental influence is followed by the influence of neighbors, church, and school. Eventually we are influenced by a multi-faceted environment that continually changes with time. We too must change and grow as the environments change and grow. To achieve that growth with stability, we must begin to realize that the multi-faceted environment includes our internal environment that starts with our cells, the smallest living unit in our system. We can shape our lives environmentally because we control the environment within us.

Biology: At our creation an egg and sperm join together to form our first cell. That one cell then divides into two other cells and each cell divides into two other cells until trillions of cells are formed. Our skin, hair, and bones and all other parts of our minds and bodies are cells. Each cell contains the same genetic code received from the egg and sperm. The code, DNA, controls life in each cell. DNA, along with the nutrients, oxygen, and hormones, determines the quality of protein and enzyme production. The quality of protein and enzymes produced determines our well-being and joy. To shape our lives, we must become aware of the effects of our thoughts and actions on the production by our body. We control the tools of production for our own bodily manufacturing plant.

By becoming more aware of how these twelve forces shape our lives, we can begin again to redefine who we are and how we do what we do.

When we blend the twelve components and form a better balanced composite, we introduce into our lives an element of being and an element of doing that are rich with potential. When having is mixed with no less than equal portions of being and doing, we have the opportunity to reach our maximum potential. From the answer to who we are comes the element of being. From the answer to what we do comes the element of doing. When being and doing become as significant in our lives as having, we have the tools we need to navigate and reach our destiny. No one can chart our course, because there is no one who is identical to us. Each of us has been given the power to chart an accurate course. But if we depend on having alone, we will have only more goods. If we combine being, doing, and having, we have a chance to develop as a whole human being.

Our lives should be lived as though we are on a treasure hunt, with all the interest and excitement that this conveys. Every one of us has a treasure that we must discover. While we are in search of our treasure, we will receive the answers we need to discover it. Once we discover the treasure, we will receive everything that we need to enjoy it to its maximum potential. In this way, all that we have flows from what we are and from what we do. Each of us has a unique talent, which is a gift from birth. Our responsibility is to use that talent to help build a great new world and to contribute so others may discover their own gift. Each of us must recognize and develop that talent. When we are working toward its attainment we feel good and we are filled with positive feelings. When we go off course we feel down and we are filled with negative feelings.

Take a blank piece of paper and begin to draw a trail of where you have been and what you have done in your life. Draw the trail as though you were moving along a highway. As you move along the highway, mark each significant milestone with an x and label the x. Place a fork in the highway at each point that you made a significant decision. At the fork proceed in the direction that the decision has taken you. Now draw a star at the top of the page. If you have discovered your treasure you are fortunate. Label the star. Your road map with all its twists and turns with all its detours should lead to the star. How direct is your path? Stop and analyze the route you have taken. We usually feel more joy and well-being when we are on the main road to our star. When we are on one of the many detours, we usually remember more pain and anguish.

For many the star has yet to be labeled. To label the star we must begin again to look within, questioning ourselves about what road to take to link up with our star. It's a shame if we get to the end of the road and we are miles from the star. The danger is that we will disregard the signals from our intuition and continue to plunge down the road to nowhere.

When we are on course, there is no mistaking the magnetic attraction. When we are off course the magnetic signal is weak. We become confused. We lose our way. When we are on course, we continually receive signals and prompts that mark our way. It's as though being, doing, and having define our path in three dimensions. We are propelled as though aboard an air-cushioned train traveling through a tunnel using the magnetic energy of a superconductor.

When we locate and label our star a peaceful and joyous state of mind develops. We achieve a balance between what our conscious mind wants our self-image to be and what our subconscious mind thinks we want it to be. The conscious mind is forever receiving and processing data from our senses and sending images of that data to our subconscious. The subconscious stores and acts on the images produced by the data to fulfill our perception of who we are. For instance, when we are enjoying a good comedy at the movies, the optic nerves send signals describing the various scenes to our conscious mind. Our conscious mind makes decisions about the images and sends those images along with positive emotions to the subconscious. If we get excited about watching a good comedy, the subconscious determines that this is part of our characteristics and includes that fact in our self-image. The job of the subconscious is to see that our conscious thoughts and images are made into reality. The subconscious is always trying to service our wishes. The answers to fulfill those wishes are sent back to our conscious mind via the intuition. When we get the urge to call someone or when we feel the urge to do some task, the urge is often a manifestation of the intuition. The greater our desire, the harder the subconscious works to fulfill that desire.[2]

The essence of being is the communication line from our senses to our conscious mind, from the conscious to the subconscious, and beyond, back through our intuition, and from the intuition to our conscious mind.[3]

Being is a conversation within ourselves. Being is active whether we are alone or with others. Basically it is the thought process. It is the times when we see something or we think of an idea and dwell on the thoughts it conveys. We search our future understanding or expansion of the thoughts. In private, being is often embellished with meditation in any of its forms. During discussions with others, it is that self-talk that goes on as we listen and converse. It is at times related to our current discussion, though often it is not. Generally, if we are positive thinkers, it is a pleasant part of our lives. You see, being is the segment of our lives that forms our self-image. It is where our self-esteem is developed. If we have a good self-image, we probably enjoy being alone and creating new things. When we have a strong self-image, we have a healthy conscious-to-subconscious connection. Our intuition is active and vibrant. Our direct line to the universal energy is open and responsive.

The Supreme Being contains all the energy required to hold all the planets in place around the sun, to hold our solar system in place, and to hold all galaxies in place in the universe. It contains all knowledge and truth. It flows through all of us as it flows through all things in the universe. To solve our problems, to reach a goal, we lock onto this energy and focus it on our need, with a simple question or conversation or self-talk. By focusing inward, we close the loop between our conscious thinking and sightings and our intuition.

Like any other part of our mind or body, our communication line must be exercised regularly to be most efficient and effective. There is a two-way flow. Energy flows inward with questions or desires from our conscious mind to our subconscious mind and beyond. Energy flows back through our subconscious to our conscious mind in the form of answers or in the form of happenings to fulfill our questions or desires.

Most of us are using less than our full potential. We have limited our world to a thought and answer process with our conscious mind and with other human beings. Most questions to which we need answers are directed to other human beings, who are often using only a small portion of their potential. They can provide an answer based only on their perception of truth, knowledge, and wisdom. Their knowledge has been derived from a different set of data and from a different perspective.

As more and more people unlock their subconscious minds, the world will see a surge of opportunity and growth rarely seen before. More and more mysteries and puzzles will be solved with clarity and conciseness. Twenty minutes of being is worth hours of doing and having. Our mind is like a computer. If we put things in motion while being it can, like a computer, be processed off-line in the background. A computer can process thousands of pieces of data instantaneously, but generally only one piece of data is accessed at any one time. When we learn to activate being in its most powerful form, we can become adept at finding answers to several questions simultaneously. Questions and desires in our minds are processed off-line and manifest themselves day by day.

One of the mental blockages to more effective being is the belief that there are finite limitations to all our resources on earth such as fuel and food, as well as to our individual abilities to bring about change. We have lost our way in many respects because we have forgotten or misinterpreted or do not believe the teachings of the great spiritual leaders of all religions. The reality of limitations is there are no limitations except those placed by man. We are blessed with great abundance. There are no limits to the earth's resources or to the material available to man. Our beliefs set our limitations and are derived from our immersion in a world of having.

This belief in the limits of society and the limits of individuals has propelled us to work harder, to do more, to produce more, to consume more. It's as though we are driven to get more of our share now rather than just getting what we need now. Our policy of maximizing production seems diametrically opposed to our view of the finite limit of resources.

The belief in limitations is growing stronger. It is driving our society to increase industrial production to overcome those limitations. It drives us to wars over resources. The more we strive individually or as a society, the more limited the solution appears.

We all thought food would be limited due to our decreasing farmland. Yet, food is more plentiful than ever. Vegetables are being grown in greenhouses row upon row going as high as man can imagine and producing all he will ever need. We believe that fuel is limited due to the finite amount of oil, yet solar energy and fusion are not far behind. Both of these will propel us to distances and places unimaginable twenty or thirty years ago. The only limitations are those that we set. There is only the scarcity that we produce. Man has always unlocked the doors necessary to take the next step, to fill a perceived need or a strong desire.

To begin to let our own personal abundance flow, we must begin to unlock and open the closed doors in our mind. These doors block the flow of abundance and create our limitations. The answers are not out there. The answers are within us. There is a great abundance. We must begin to accept that abundance as our natural state. It comes from being.

Once we begin to accept abundance as reality in our lives, the things we need to do are clearer and simpler. Once we accept the view of abundance, the need for comparison and competition decreases. We then spend our time and energy doing activities that contribute to our well-being and to the well-being of others. Doing comes much more easily.

By being, first, we leave the house with many of the answers we need for the day. By being, first, we will realize that much of the difficulties added to our day's chores were put there by our beliefs and perceptions.

Doing is the activity in life that stems from all the creative energy we have. This is the part of our life where we pursue our career, where we perform the tasks that will give us all the things we would have. From doing comes the opportunity to create wealth and abundance and all the good things in life. The key ingredient to doing is quality.

Doing becomes for the most part a daily routine. We are repetitive creatures who become comfortable in a routine that provides the discipline in itself. If our employer tells us to eat lunch at noon each day, we accept that discipline. It is a discipline built in for us. We don't have to think each day of when we are going to go to lunch. If our lunch is provided each day, that is great because we do not have to decide each day where or what we are going to eat. We are comfortable with discipline from outside.

In general, doing our daily tasks, exercising, eating, and resting are scheduled for us. We can devote more time to performing creative discretionary tasks with quality. The quality of our actions will determine the quality of our lives. For instance, if we eat properly, our health is more robust. With more robust health comes a higher quality of life. The same is true of quality in our work, quality in our exercise, quality in our play, and quality in our rest. Each builds on our mental and physical health, which lets us enjoy life to the maximum.

Doing should, for greatest success, be completed in the most effortless way. Man is always striving to invent machines and gadgets to make work easier. Work is more satisfying, it seems, when we complete the task with a tired feeling free of the element of stress. Did you ever notice when you worked at home by yourself or with a friend on a weekend that you ended the day with a good tired feeling. When we sit back after a day of painting at home, we find that although we are tired, we are also relaxed. Did you ever notice what a great tired feeling you have at the end of the day from cross-country or downhill skiing? Skiing, for most of us, uses more energy than anything else we do all week, but we feel great doing it.

If we go about doing our tasks without much thought or with countless interruptions, our minds are forced to jump back and forth from distraction to distraction. This makes us feel stressed and stress tires. If we don't stop and think before we do a task, we don't bring all our brainpower to bear on that one task. Therefore, like a machine required to start and stop to do several things instead of one, we are not able to work at peak efficiency. We work at peak efficiency when we apply maximum brainpower or thought to what we do. We are most efficient when we think before we act. We are most efficient when we bring in an element of being before doing.

To accomplish a goal, any goal, with maximum efficiency, we must first perceive or visualize the end result. Each task becomes easier when we have a plan. A plan lets us visualize each step of a project from beginning to end. Now we have the start and the finish line clearly in mind. By introducing the element of being to help us plan and visualize, the tasks between the start and the finish line are much easier. We focus better because we know where we are going and, therefore, we proceed without introducing that element of stress known as the unknown.

Being makes doing a pleasure. We think, we plan, we see the finish line clearly. The implementation requires only that we follow our road map. Did you ever go on a trip where you had never been to your destination, where you had not bothered to think before you started out, and where you had not bothered to look at a map? What a mistake. We introduce a degree of stress that makes the trip a chore. We get there tired. We don't see the finish line. We don't have a plan and once we drive past the area with which we are familiar, we are constantly anticipating. That is why a trip always seems longer when we are driving to a new destination than when we are returning home.

In everything we do, we have the opportunity to change the journey from pain to pleasure. All we need to do is visualize the finish line in our mind. Introduce being. We must visualize how we are going to get there and plan the journey. With a plan, every trip is easier. We will minimize stress and anticipation.

Despite our view that limitations exist, our society has made much progress and our lives have been filled with more abundance than those of other civilizations to date. Our leisure time has increased as our work week has decreased and many industries have sprung up to create ways to help us spend our leisure hours. We are a very active society. However, we do sense that something is missing. The fulfillment from our work and play does not seem to be complete, though it is the best that anyone has developed to date.

Somehow our career and our playtime do not quite provide the quality and the pleasure that we expected. Now in fact we are concerned that perhaps we have peaked as a society. Despite the introduction of supercomputers with superspeed that can process countless amounts of information and free us from many repetitive tasks, our work week is again increasing. To make ends meet, two incomes are required in most families. Fifty percent of women have joined the work force. The sentence, "There has to be a better way to make a living," is becoming more and more prevalent. Our tasks are requiring greater energy than we hoped.

We bet too much on having. As man invented machines at an ever faster pace, we became the slaves of those machines. Productivity depended on keeping those machines going for as many hours as humanly possible. Increased quantity of goods depended on more productivity, faster lines, more goods flowing to market, more purchases by consumers, more consumption by users. The entire loop fueled itself in a closed loop manner, until the increased consumption required an increase in the number of machines, and an increase in the number of hours worked, more goods again, and more consumption. Has all this increase increased our degree of happiness? Some will argue yes; it has increased our happiness to a certain degree. We have more material goods to fill our basic needs than ever before. We are not required to work for survival only. The basics come easily. We have time for leisure and we have extra cash to buy the good things--that bottle of fine wine, the supplies for our weekend picnics, the vacation at our favorite get-away spot. On a daily basis we can turn on the TV or listen to our favorite. We see more sports tapes activity in one week than we once saw in a month. We can play more golf and tennis. We drive our cars with more joy and pleasure on highways that take us to any place in less time than before.

With all this, however, our society seems to have reached a plateau. We seem to be in search of something more. What is that nagging empty feeling? What is that yearning? All these material goods, though pleasant and enjoyable, don't quite fulfill it.

Erich Fromm in his book <u>To Have or To Be</u>? asks, "If I am what I have and if what I have is lost, who then am I?"[4] We must be more than what we have. We must be. Having is not an end in itself. Having is the means to the end. It's only the beginning. It gets us to the starting line. We must traverse from the starting line to the goal line and then start again and reach the next goal line and the next goal line. The game can go on forever. There is no end to the number of goal lines you can reach. There are no limitations. Having provides us with the abundance of goods to carry us as far as we want to go. It is the propellant, and if used properly it will build and build on itself so we can always strive to reach great heights.

By having a certain amount of success materially we can quiet the basic needs in us. When we satisfy our basic needs, we can begin to contribute to more noble needs of our society. Material success gives us time to investigate and experiment. It gives us cash to purchase the products for experiments. It gives us the capacity to improve the value of our nutrition. It quiets the spirit so love may surface. But having the material goods doesn't guarantee that we will find fulfillment. It will provide us with the time and energy to find fulfillment.

To be what we want to be, however, requires that we change the order of our lives. Our life will assume a balance, a peace with harmony when we change the order to first being, then doing, and then having.

One example of using being, doing, and having in consort is when we head for the beach or a lake on a Saturday morning. We feel so free. All the week's responsibilities are behind us. We get into our beautiful automobile and we drive away from all our cares. All our aches and pains are forgotten. We pick up our best friend. The talk comes easily. Laughter comes easily. We focus on one thing--the day. We arrive at the beach and we begin to move more slowly. We admire the bright shining sun. We scan and admire the long sandy beach. We watch all those beautiful people "doing their thing." All day long our mind floats back and forth between being, doing, and having. Our picnic lunch is perfect.

We pull out a good book and read with ease and understanding. We doze off for a good hour--oblivious to the events around us. We wake up, feel refreshed, and go for a long walk or jog along the beach. We have more energy. Answers to questions long forgotten pop into our heads.

Those days are heaven on earth, our Garden of Eden. They are the times when we are at picnics and weddings. We get along with everyone. We communicate with ease. We love. We share. We enjoy being with people. Everyone is so relaxed and giving. Nothing seems impossible. We believe we can achieve anything we want. It is truly magnificent.

We can learn to sustain those days if we introduce being into our lives and begin again, clearing away false beliefs and failed truths. We can sustain those days if we raise our awareness, change, and grow. We can sustain those days by revisiting the twelve components that shape our lives and by defining our own core of truths. Let us start the journey now and visit twelve of the components that shape our lives.

CHAPTER 2

LOOKING WITHIN

To improve our lives from within, we must become aware that all our thoughts and all our actions affect who we are and how we feel. By modifying those thoughts and actions, we are free to change who we are and how we feel. Thoughts affect our well-being by affecting the quality of the hormones we generate and by affecting the quality of the nerve impulses transmitted to all parts o. Actions affect our well f our minds and bodies -being through the quality of nutrients we provide and through the oxygen we provide during periods of vigorous exercise, moderate activity, and rest.

Much has been written by people such as Norman Vincent Peale, Dale Carnegie, Zig Zigler, and many others on the impact of positive and negative thinking on our health. The basis of their theories is that our psychological and physical activity translates to our biological state. What we think and do is eventually translated into some chemical and electrical process in our minds and bodies. These processes are transmitted from the psychological and physical by the biofeedback mechanisms in our system. The quality of those processes determines the abundance of energy and enthusiasm in our lives. Each of us controls the tools of production that generate those processes. The tools of production biologically are the nutrients, oxygen, and hormones that combine with coded data in our cells. Energy and enthusiasm are the end products of the tools of production.

Biologically we are all unique. Of the billions of people who have populated the earth, no two have been alike. It is the responsibility of each of us to reach an understanding of who we are and to use the tools of production to maximize our individual potential.

21

The brain is the control center of our minds and body. It receives all external information through our five senses--sight, smell, hearing, taste and touch, and through the millions of receptors on our skin. The brain is at the center of the many biofeedback control systems. When we are too hot, for instance, the receptors on our skin send signals back to the brain. The brain takes the signals and goes to work to produce the chemical and electrical impulses that generates sweat. The sweat pours out of our skin and cools our body. Receptors in the skin send back signals saying the body has cooled and the brain reacts by cutting off the production of sweat. There are hundreds of such systems in our body. They are known to us as hunger pains, thirst, energy for jogging, digestion, emptying the bladder, and so on.

One branch of medicine has formed to use biofeedback to control the body's functions in order to cure itself. Patients are trained to control their thought process to focus on the pain or the symptom of a particular organ, which will send healing signals to that area. In one book on biofeedback, New Mind, New Body, Dr. Barbara B. Brown describes how skin talk communicates with the mind to produce signals to be acted on by the brain. Lie detector tests are based on this communication link between skin surface and the brain.[1] In general, biofeedback is the principle behind the generation of oxygen, nutrients, and hormones to each cell. A change in our internal environment initiates the activity. The brain responds and issues a signal to dampen the change. For instance, one internal change may require water to be provided to the cells. The brain generates a signal of thirst. We respond by drinking a glass of water. The fluid is digested, sent through the bloodstream, and used by the cells. When the body has received enough, signals are sent back to dampen the signal of thirst. The biofeedback dampens the signal to zero and our thirst disappears.

To improve from within we can improve our response to our biofeedback system. One area that we have all strived to improve is our memories. Some have a knack for remembering people's names and others forget a name two minutes after it has been heard. But almost everyone who has tried to improve memory has succeeded.

On the first night of a Dale Carnegie memory improvement course, the instructor has everyone (usually twenty to thirty people) give their name. When the names have been given, the instructor asks each person to repeat all the names. Only one or two people usually can repeat all the names. With some urging by the instructor, however, which increases the focus and concentration of the participants, the number of people able to recall the names increases dramatically. By concentrating and focusing, we zero in on that part of the mind that remembers. We stimulate and exercise that part of the mind, and the many nerve cells in that part of the mind grow stronger.

Improving reflexes or improving reaction time to some external stimulus is a way that we increase focus, exercise the mind, and improve the nervous system transmission through the neurons or nerve cells.

Picture the first time you tried to hit a baseball: The eyes have to register the baseball coming from the pitcher's hand, transmitting a picture through the nerve in the eye to the brain. The brain has to translate the signal, gauge where the ball is going, evaluate the ball's progress every second, and transmit signals throughout the arms and legs to coordinate a swing or an attack on the approaching baseball. Our first attempts at doing this are dismal. We swing, but we miss aiming high or low by as much as a foot. Over time, with great focus and concentration, we are able to actually foul off a few pitches and we feel great satisfaction. We have trained our eyes and limbs to coordinate this activity. With more practice, we are able to hit the ball as though it is second nature. We expect to hit the ball.

Learning to ride a bicycle involves the same process and focus until the brain is coordinating all necessary bicycle-riding muscles and senses in unison. At the beginning, we fall every three feet or every revolution of the pedal. In time, usually with great parental assistance and urging, we ride with ease. Our brain has taken over and constructed a team made up of bicycle-riding muscles and senses. The required balance is taken for granted.

Biofeedback uses the same control system mechanism that we use to hit a baseball or to ride a bicycle. In fact these are biofeedback systems. But biofeedback in medicine teaches us to focus and concentrate internally. We focus on a particular muscle set or on a particular organ or system. We must become as adept at receiving and sending signals internally as we are at receiving and sending signals externally. That is, we must learn to send back the thoughts and actions that will provide a positive stimulus to each part of our minds and bodies. Of course thousands of signals are automatically received and sent internally every minute. But if we are able to learn to hit a baseball or ride a bike, we should be capable of focus and concentration to improve ourselves internally.

When we heal an area of our body in pain, we are healing the cells that have become damaged or we are replacing the cells that have died. This process goes on automatically each day. Cells are programmed to live days or weeks or years. Skin cells die and are replaced daily. Nerve cells are an exception. They do not reproduce. But they are plentiful enough to last a lifetime and they are programmed to live our full lifetime and beyond.[2]

Cells are the eventual recipients of our biofeedback activity. Cells are the ultimate beneficiaries, for better or for worse, of our thoughts and actions. All our thoughts and actions define the stability of what has been called our homeostatis' environment. How stable that environment is maintained determines how effectively the cells can produce.

We are created from one cell. That first cell is created in union between the egg from our mother and the sperm from our father. Each additional cell is formed when the first cell and subsequent cells divide and become two. When all division is completed and we have reached our physical peak, somewhere between late adolescence and adulthood, we are made of trillions of cells. When the first cell is created from the egg and sperm, we inherit from our parents a genetic code, which remains in the nucleus of each cell throughout our lives. These cells make up our skin, our hair, our organs, and all other parts of our minds and bodies. How we treat these cells determines how well we function.

Most of our conscious effort in maintaining our health is spent on the surface. We shower each day to stay clean. We brush our teeth to keep them clean and white. We shave to keep our faces clean and smooth. We wash and prep our hair to make it clean and attractive. We apply skin moisturizers and tanning lotion to look young and fit.

But to shape our lives biologically and environmentally we must become more aware of the impact of our thoughts and actions internally.

Picture trillions of cells inside our body. One hundred thousand of these cells fit on the head of a pin. Now assume that all cells are trying to take a shower at the same time. This would require a good water supply and we would depend on the bloodstream to provide all that water. After each cell cleanses itself it would expel all the waste back into the bloodstream. The bloodstream would carry the waste to intestines to the kidneys and bladder and out of the body.

If we did not provide enough water, the cells could not clean themselves. The waste would remain in the cell and the cell would deteriorate. Think of how our body feels when you need a shower after you have played volleyball for hours. What if you did not have any water? What if you went without a shower for two or three weeks? We must provide enough water internally to cleanse ourselves as thoroughly as we cleanse ourselves externally. We must become aware of how our thoughts and actions affect our body internally.

Visualize each cell as though it were shaped like a chicken's egg. On the outside of the cell is a membrane somewhat more porous than the shell of an egg. Inside the membrane are two parts of the cell--a nucleus similar to the yellow yoke of the egg, and a complementary part surrounding the yoke similar to the egg white. The genetic code received from our parents is housed in the nucleus of each cell.

The genetic code is hereditary. From that code we inherit characteristics of our father and mother. Our eye and hair color is similar to that of one parent. Our skin is of the same texture and color of one parent. We often resemble one parent in physical appearance. Our manner of walking and talking is often very similar to that of one parent. The genetic code contains the instructions that are used by our minds and bodies to grow from conception to adulthood and to reach full physical maturity.

These instructions are carried on two sets of chromosomes, one set from each parent. We are all somewhat like our parents, but we are all different. We differ so widely because each parent provided us with only one half of his or her chromosomes and because of the thousands of combinations possible between egg and sperm at conception.

At conception we are near perfection. Equal quantities of genetic instructions come from the mother and the father. The nucleus of the egg from the mother contains twenty-three chromosomes, each carrying a different part instructions. The sperm cell nucleus from the father also contains twenty-three chromosomes, carrying a similar set of instructions. During fertilization, the two nuclei merge into one having forty-six chromosomes. So the fertilized egg contains two sets of instructions, one from the mother and one from the father. The chromosomes in the fertilized egg carry the instructions for all the cells that make up the body. As the cell develops it divides over and over again and an exact copy of all the instructions is passed to each cell. The forty-six chromosomes form twenty-three pairs of chromosomes in the nucleus of every cell. With one exception, the two chromosomes in each pair look the same and carry the same genetic instructions. The one chromosome pair that is different determines our sex. This is the only genetic difference between male and female. The twenty-third pair contains what is called an x chromosome and a y chromosome. The female pair has two x's, while the male pair has an x and a y.

What do the chromosomes determine? They determine the genetic makeup of DNA (deoxyribonucleic acid). The DNA determines how all parts of our bodies are to be formed. The chromosomes through DNA reproduce themselves from the one cell into trillions of cells. Some cells become part of bone, some cells become part of muscle, and some become part of tissue.

DNA has two important functions. The first is to reproduce itself in cells prior to the division of each cell into two new cells. The second is to apply its code to the shaping of specific protein molecules that make up the body of the cell, directing the reproduction and growth of each living cell.

Intricate chemical reactions take place within the cell to release the DNA code from the nucleus to the body of the cell. The protein molecule that is formed by DNA is formed from the twenty amino acids that we include in our diet. The DNA code designates which of the twenty amino acids to form at any one time. The amino acids can form up to 100,000 various protein used in the body. One by one, following the exact order laid down by the DNA code, the proper amino acids are brought into line and welded into a chain.

The most vital protein produced are enzymes. Enzymes are the catalytic agent in the biological processes.

Enzymes break down protein from the food we eat to make free amino acids as required by the DNA code. Hormones start the process in the cell. Enzymes control the activity inside the cell.

The formation of protein takes place in that section of the cell between nucleus and membrane. Nutrients, oxygen, and hormones are brought in from the bloodstream through the membrane. DNA is brought in from the nucleus. The membrane keeps out harmful substances, but allows nutritious substances to enter the cell. Waste products and materials made by the cell are allowed to pass out through the membrane into the bloodstream. How well we feel is dependent on the quality of the nutrients we provide to each cell and how well we provide all the vitamins and minerals it needs to maintain its health.

As a baby grows into an adult, the number of cells in its body increases. The visible effect of this cell multiplication can be seen as increases in weight and height. Its shape and body proportion all change in accordance with the instructions. When a cell is about to divide, it takes in nourishment and grows to twice its original size. The membrane around the nucleus disappears and a furrow starts to form around the cell. The nucleus divides in two, and the furrow around the cell gradually deepens, eventually splitting the cell into two new cells. Even in an adult, cells in many parts of the body need to grow and divide to replace their dead and dying neighbors. And cells that cannot be replaced need to be kept in working order.

Water and protein are the most prevalent substances in each cell. Water is 70 percent of the solution. Protein is 10-20 percent. There are many different kinds of cells, each designed to do a particular job. For instance, when food is digested, it must be absorbed into the bloodstream so that it can provide nutrition to all the cells in the body. Cells designated for that task line the small intestine. Digested food is absorbed from the intestine through the cell membrane into the cell and passed out the lower membrane of the cell into the bloodstream to be transported to other cells. In like fashion, various cells and cell structures perform all the activities necessary to maintain life, including respiration, digestion, excretion, and reproduction. The cell is the smallest living unit in our bodies. It transforms the nutrients into energy, grows, and reproduces.

Each group of cells constitutes a tissue such as muscle and bone. The tissue in turn compose organs such as stomach, kidney, heart, lungs, etc. Finally the organs are grouped into systems such as the cardiovascular system, the nervous system, the endocrine system, the digestive system.

Five systems in our body have a great deal to do with maintaining and stabilizing the surroundings for the cells. These are the nervous system, the respiratory system, the cardiovascular system, the digestive system, and the endocrine system. They conduct the biological transactions that keep our environment stable.

First, let's look at the nervous system. The nervous system is made up of millions of nerve cells called neurons. They differ from other cells in both appearance and behavior. They look like an octopus. One tentacle called the axon carries impulses away from the cell body. All other tentacles called dendrites receive impulses and carry them to the center of the cell. Their special shape allow them to receive, carry, and pass on signals. Of course the neurons like other cells contain DNA at the cell nucleus.

As they pass through the body, axons and dendrites are enclosed in a flexible tube to form a cable of nerve fibers. This cable is commonly called a nerve. Collectively the nerve cells control thought, feeling, and action. The nerve cells are interconnected into a vast telephone system. This vast telephone system can be divided into three parts--the central nervous system, the peripheral nervous system, and the autonomic nervous system.

The central nervous system is the brain and spinal cord. The brain is the coordinating and decision making center of our nervous system and has three parts: the cerebrum, the cerebellum and the brain stem. The cerebellum, at the base of the brain, has two main tasks--to provide sense of balance and to coordinate motion. The brain stem connects the nerve paths between the cerebrum and the spinal cord. It controls secretion and, therefore, reaction to emotion.

The cerebrum is the largest part of the brain and is the seat of the mind. It has two halves, which are called the cerebral hemispheres. In most people, the left hemisphere is dominant, resulting in a larger number of right-handed than left-handed people.

The more developed the cerebral hemisphere becomes as a result of experience and knowledge, the greater the alternatives of behavior -- perception increases, reasoning deepens, and the conscious level of the mind broadens.

The peripheral nervous system through the spinal cord flows signals from the brain to the outer body structure such as the muscles and skin. Receptors convert all kinds of information from outside our body and send this information to the brain.

The autonomic nervous system consists of glands and nerves which control all the involuntary organs such as heart, kidney, stomach, and intestines.

The nervous system is the most critical system in our body, running from the mind to every other part of our body. It is working every second to sense and receive data from our surroundings. It receives signals through every part of our skin as in sensing hot and cold around our body. It receives signals of our surroundings through our eyes, nose, ears, and mouth. It absorbs knowledge, thoughts, and energy through the mind.

The nervous system in conjunction with the digestive system, the respiratory system, the cardiovascular system, and the endocrine system controls the flow to and from the cells. One of the primary functions of these systems is to maintain our surroundings so that each cell may thrive and, therefore, that as a total of all cells, we may thrive.

The digestive system receives and processes the food and drink that we consume and passes all nutrients through the small intestines into the bloodstream for use by the cells. It also processes all waste from the bloodstream out of the body. The digestive system starts at the lips and ends at the anus. It includes the esophagus, stomach, intestines, liver, pancreas, and gall bladder. Enzymes produced by the cells are sent to the digestive system to break down the food into the nutrients that are needed by the cells. The enzymes act on the three basic food groups we provide--carbohydrates, fats, and proteins.

The respiratory system is all the breathing apparatus of nose, mouth, and lungs. The lungs convert air to oxygen and pass the oxygen to the bloodstream for use by the cells. The lungs also remove from the bloodstream one of the waste products, carbon dioxide.

The cardiovascular system consists of the heart, the pulmonary circuit, and the systemic circuit. The heart is a large muscle consisting of two pumping and two receiving chambers. The pulmonary circuit carries blood in need of oxygen to the lungs of the respiratory system and blood with oxygen back to the heart. The systemic circuit carries blood rich in nutrients and oxygen to the cells in all parts of the body and waste away from all cells in all parts of the body.

The endocrine system is a series of eight glands in the brain and body that release hormones directly into the bloodstream. The eight glands are the pituitary and pineal glands in the mind, the thyroid and parathyroid in the throat, and the pancreatic and the suprarenal in the stomach region, and two each in either the testes for males and ovaries for females. Hormones regulate the cell activity in other parts of the body. When some thought or action stimulates the production of a hormone, the hormone corrects an imbalance and eliminates the need for the stimulus. Therefore, it acts as a biofeedback control system. Hormones coordinate body activities, control growth and development, and maintain a stable environment for the cells. The endocrine system interacts with the nervous system to bring about various responses to stimuli in our external and internal environment. Our thoughts and actions have a great effect on the generation of the hormones. Hormones control the permeability of the cell membrane, and activate DNA in the nucleus of the cell to produce protein.

The five systems working together would look something like the view in Figure 2-1.

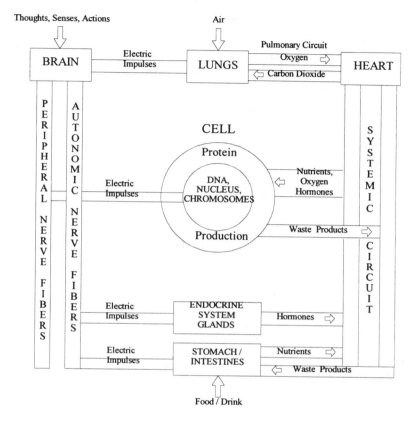

Figure 2-1

The health of the body is affected by our ability to provide the trillions of cells in our body with a stable internal environment. We do this by providing good food and plenty of water, by providing clean air, and by exercising and by resting properly. We also do this by raising our awareness through education, by maintaining a healthy vibrant external environment at school, at work and at home, by developing our direct spiritual line, by creating through play, by freeing ourselves of fears and phobias, and by using our material

31

rewards to contribute to the love and well-being of our neighbors. All thoughts and actions affect us biologically.

Improvement in each area improves the quality of our thoughts and actions. Through a raised awareness the quality of our thoughts and actions helps us form new beliefs grounded more firmly in truth, more closely aligned to who we are, to what we truly want to be and do. Our thoughts and actions shape the nerve cell patterns in our brain. The rest of the nervous system translates those patterns and transmits vibrant impulses throughout our mind and body for better protein production and more energy generation by the cells. How successful we are in the dynamic generation of energy is a major factor in determining how much well-being, joy, and happiness will fill our lives.

CHAPTER 3

CREATING STABILITY

After our birth, biological influences are joined by environmental influences. We are shaped by everything around us. We observe people and objects and we absorb like a sponge. Our observations are sent by our senses to our conscious mind. The conscious mind sends the most powerful thoughts to our subconscious. The subconscious uses these environmental influences to shape our self-image and our behavior.

In our early life, our parents, with whom we spend almost all our time, try to provide us with stability in which we can grow and flourish. During those years our sense of what is biological or hereditary is blurred with what is environmental because almost everything in early life has to do with parents.

Then when we venture outside the home, we are exposed to a wider environment. Our environmental influences continue to expand when we start school, when we go to church, and when we participate in community activities. Eventually our horizons expand until we sense and are affected by the environments of school, neighborhood, community, country, state, region, country, Western or Eastern civilization, earth, and universe. How do we cope with a multi-faceted, multi-dimensional environment that is constantly changing? We do this by developing and maintaining a stable internal environment.

Our internal environment must be as adaptable as that of a tree. The internal environment of a tree adapts despite adverse external conditions. The tree always adjusts despite wild swings in temperature and sunlight. In the springtime, prodded by warm showers and increasing sunlight, the tree blooms. Through the long hot days of summer, leaves grow and flourish on its branches. In the fall, cooling temperatures and decreasing sunlight causes the leaves to change colors.

Finally, in late fall the tree releases all leaves. In winter, during days with the coldest temperatures and least amount of sunlight, the tree rests and rejuvenates. In the spring, growth begins again. Despite the harshness of change, trees may live for many years through all seasons. They adapt and change internally to meet the external changes. Given clean air, rain, and minerals from the soil, each tree grows stronger and repeats the cycle continuously.

To smooth our way we must become aware that our environmental influences are not limited to those of home or neighborhood or town. To find the right path for our journey, we must recognize that our environmental influences start at the very core of our being. For maximum success we must value the influences of our internal environment at least to the same degree as we value the influences of our external environment.

By using the intuitive flow from within, we can learn to be more selective of the influences in our external environment. When we are busy keeping up with the friends and neighbors, we are living with the influence of our external environment. Without benefit of our own promptings from within, we are pursuing someone else's idea of living. However, we are all different. There is nothing external that can provide the full guidance and inspiration we need. To maximize our potential, we must learn to have our thoughts and actions flow from our own subconscious to the conscious. We must cultivate the ability to become quiet externally so that our thoughts may surface from within. Any desire presented externally for fulfillment will be tempered by the agenda and desires of others. A healthy vibrant internal environment will let our thoughts surface to fill any desire.

Figure 2-1 in Chapter 2, presents a schematic of how we maintain stability in our lives by generating the proper hormones, by inhaling clean air, and by eating the proper nutrients. All of this benefits the millions of cells in our mind and body. To shape ourselves environmentally we must become aware that every cell within us is part of our environment. How we treat the cells determines the stability of our environment.

Claude Bernard, the famous French physiologist introduced the term "internal environment."[1] The American physiologist Walter Cannon extended the concept to a constant internal environment and coined the term homeostasis. Homeostasis states that to function properly, cells require constant environment.

To maintain that constant internal environment, the mind and body work together through biofeedback. Based on signals transmitted throughout the body by the nervous and endocrine systems, blood content and pressure are kept constant, heartbeat is adjusted, body temperature is stabilized, and body fluid level and content are monitored and adjusted.

The most obvious effect that we have on our internal environment is through the quality of the food that we select to eat and the quality of the air that we breathe. We select food that we enjoy and next we consider its nutritional value. If a food tastes bad to our palate, we avoid that food. This avoidance is a filter or screen for what we take into our system. If the sun is too bright, we squint or close our eyes, filtering out the light. We receive inputs to our internal environment through many parts of the body. Our skin is full of receptors that tell our mind that it is cold or hot. Our eyes, ears, and nose are constantly receiving inputs, which are fed back to the mind for evaluation.

One of the most dramatic impacts to our internal environment occurs when we consume an excess of coffee or alcohol. Our entire nervous system (brain, peripheral, and autonomic) is affected. The withdrawal from either coffee or alcohol causes an excess of impulses to be transmitted through the nerve fibers. These extraneous impulses dampen the ability of the nervous system to transmit signals for normal body functions. We are unable to sense properly, thru our biofeedback system. Our system then operates open loop. We feel unprotected and vulnerable. These feelings arise even while our external environments are constant and quiet. We modify our behavior because of the imbalance in our internal environment. Our thoughts and actions do not become rational until the nervous system balance is restored and the electrical, chemical, and biological processes return to normal levels.

The same effect is created when drugs are ingested. Our internal environment becomes unbalanced. The cells in the nervous system of mind and body cannot produce the proper electrical, chemical, and biological signals. Without the proper signals, hormones cannot be produced in the proper amounts. Nutrients cannot be produced as efficiently from the food we eat. The air we breathe cannot be converted to normal levels of oxygen. We introduce blockages in the nervous system that interfere with a rational conscious and unconscious thought process. Not until these drugs can be washed into the digestive tract and out of our body can the blockages be cleared and normal processing return.

For the vast majority of the time that we are in a harmful state, that is in a state of unbalance in our internal environment, the cause is internal, from our own thoughts and actions. On a few occasions, the imbalance is caused by sudden and unexpected crises outside our control, perhaps by a natural phenomenon such as an earthquake, or a tornado, or perhaps by someone outside our circle of control. But even external crises must be resolved from within.

Sometime when your system is at peace, take a moment to look at the world from inside yourself. Form an image in your mind of yourself as though you are a whole person looking outside from your mind to the world around you. Now visualize that whole person looking out at the rest of the world. Remember you are at peace. You've taken nothing that upsets your system. As you look round your world, everything should look clear and bright. The sun cascades across mountain tops and hillsides. Clean water runs through the valleys. You feel optimistic. Everything you see, you see as an opportunity. Everyone you see you see as a friend. Continue looking out in this peaceful state. You walk down Main Street with a jaunty step. People wave. You feel good, as if you can accomplish any goal. Every challenge that steps in your path is resolved easily. You look forward to seeing friends. You want to exchange greetings and share the day's news.

Now take this same view of the world, but insert a level of anxiety in your mind. Recall the anxiety created when you drink too much coffee or alcohol. Now look around again. Things look hazy and shaky. Clouds fill the sky. The water is filled with pollutants. Everything seems to be a chore. No one likes you. You drag yourself down Main Street and wish you were somewhere else. You just don't feel like doing anything. Everything and everyone you see increases your anxiety level.

Two views of the same world from one person appear as two different worlds. The external environment in both views is the same, but appears different. The differences are caused by the change in stability of the internal environment. One internal environment breeds confidence and optimism. Another internal environment breeds fear and pessimism.

If we were to take a walk in our minds through ten or twenty different external environments, the results would always be the same. When our internal environment is healthy, stable, and steady, we can conquer every obstacle, and make every goal, and fulfill every dream. When our internal environment is unbalanced and shaky we are blocked by every obstacle, fall short of every goal, and miss every opportunity.

The internal environment is our key to success. If we nurture and build our mind, body, and soul, nothing outside of us can beat us. With a strong mind, body, and soul, we can receive all the knowledge we need and possess the best judgment to meet every situation. The stronger we get internally, the more we can accomplish externally.

Everyone has the same opportunity to guide his or her own destiny through nurturing the internal environment. The thoughts and actions that we filter through our senses define the quality of our life.

We are all presented with hundreds of choices across a broad spectrum of opportunities from diverse cultures. The selections we make, the ideas we embrace, the opportunities we pursue are a reflection of what drives us internally. The quality of these choices is based on the quality of our senses, our thoughts, and our actions. If our senses and thoughts can screen the opportunities accurately, we make good choices that build on themselves and strengthen us for bolder selections and wiser decisions.

If the multiple external environments and the change in each were a threat to man, the changes we have encountered through the twentieth century would have reduced the entire human race to a "basket case." Yet the opposite has happened. The human race and individual human beings have grown and prospered.

Let's look at some of the changes that have taken place in our external environment in this century. In the early 1900s, we shifted from an agricultural society to an industrialized one. To achieve the greatest mass production required that we go from a decentralized society to a centralized one.

In the agricultural society, there was much individuality. People practiced specialized craftsmanship. Some were shoesmiths, some made leather goods, some farmed the land. The direction from a federal government was minimal. People governed themselves through town meetings.

Then came the production machines of the industrial society. To put these machines in action, the people were attracted from the farms and towns to the cities. Red brick buildings were constructed for miles to house the workers and machines. This was viewed as progress. Mass production was the prime concept behind industrialization. To meet the economic goals of mass production, the federal government began playing a more active role. The population became centralized in the cities. Economic policy became centralized in Washington. Individuality gave way to conformity. Standard work hours and work weeks were set. Multiple shifts were organized to keep the machines working. People adjusted and talked of the good life. To run the machines, which became more sophisticated, better educated workers were required. Education became more critical in the life-style of the people. Most everyone's level of knowledge and awareness had to be raised. The external environment changed rapidly. Along came automobiles, airplanes, and radio. Then came computers, microwaves, and VCRs. Many saw change as an opportunity. Some saw change as threatening. But for the most part, the changes in the environment were taken in stride. The level of education increased the level of awareness and knowledge. Education made people accept the new machines and take them in as part of their expected lifestyle. Without education to understand what had happened and what was happening, society and the majority of individuals would have been destabilized.

Now, society is going through a change as significant as the change from agriculture to industrialization. We are passing from industrialization with mass production to customization. Society, within boundary limitations set by the increased population, will pass from centralization to decentralization. People have attained such a high level of awareness that they now can act as individuals while in a centralized setting. The variety of acceptable choices allows individuality to flourish once again.

The evidence is all around us. Customization can be seen in the increasing number of new businesses and in the increased amount of self-employment. It can be seen in the movement from city to suburbs, in the increase of and dependence on the automobile, in computer networks. Customization is to stress one's individuality in each facet of life and to develop in accordance with individual specifications. When practiced in its highest form, customization breeds creativity. Individuals must create what is unique for them, in order to meet their unique individual requirements and expectations.

Customization in industry is fueled by robotics. When robotics reaches its potential, individuals will select a customized product from a computer terminal at the start of the assembly line and the flexibility of computers, computer software, and robotics will manufacture each new product to different specifications and to individual final designs. Customization in industry will allow use of computer networks to decentralize the workplace. More and more people will work in home offices and send the finished product over fax lines or computer modems.

Customization is irreversible. Education continues to expand and create more acceptable choices. Our level of awareness provides us with a better data bank to make acceptable choices for our unique biological makeup. We have more opportunity to take in new choices and modify our self-image. As the term customization implies, these changes will make this an era of the individual. As in all other changes to our external environment, the challenge to each individual will be to maintain an internal stability.

To maintain that stability while shaping our internal environment, we must find ways to improve physically and mentally. Tremendous strides are being made through the study of genetics. New drugs are coming out almost daily to treat illness. New discoveries on the effects of nutrients and hormones on our vitality are being made almost daily.

If we raise our level of awareness and begin to provide the correct balance of carbohydrates, fats, and proteins, and we begin to provide our oxygen through healthy lungs and begin to exercise to maintain our flexibility, we can stretch our limits and our potential. Our internal environment will get better physically and mentally and this will feed on itself to allow us to make wiser decisions about our mental and physical health.

How can we measure the stability of our internal environment? Physically, body temperature, blood pressure, cholesterol level, and fat level in the blood, pulse rate, body fat content, and lung capacity are the most common measures. One typical person might have the following profile: Temperature -98.6, Pressure - 120/80, cholesterol - 200 milligrams, fat (triglycerides) - 120 milligrams, body fat - 20%, and lung capacity 85%. Blood tests and stress tests can be conducted to measure other factors in our internal environment. Psychologically, stability of our internal environment can be measured by how relaxed we are or by the amount of energy and enthusiasm we have or by the well-being, joy, and happiness we feel.

Ultimately, the best measure of the stability in our internal environment is the measure of love in our hearts. For maximum stability in our internal environment we must be no more nor less than good conductors of love. When we carry hate, fear, anger, guilt, jealousy, greed, and revenge through our nervous, endocrine, respiratory, digestive, and cardiovascular systems, we diminish the amount of love that we may conduct. This diminishes the health of all systems.

Researchers, biologists, psychologists, and other persons of science when attempting to uncover the reason for the longer life span of women would find no better place to start than in the measure of the amount of love in their hearts.

CHAPTER 4

OPENING OUR DIRECT PATH

Spirituality is the essence of being. Spirituality is one part destiny, one part meditation, one part intuition, and one part action. Spirituality is like a good game of treasure hunt. Each game leads us to our most current goal. Each succeeding game leads us to new goals. Like any game, we get the chance to start over many times until we stop playing or until we find our door to the Kingdom of Heaven. Spirituality is a win-win situation. You cannot lose, you can only refuse to play. When you win, all your friends and neighbors win. The one part destiny is our treasure, our purpose for being. One part meditation is placing questions about our treasure into our subconscious. One part intuition is the answers to those questions. One part action is putting those answers to work in our physical and intellectual activity.

When we shape our life biologically, environmentally, and spiritually we are shaping the playing field. We are clearing the pathways of debris so that the transmission between mind, body, and soul may be stronger and clearer. We all have a direct line to God that we must cultivate. When we are effective in shaping our lives biologically, environmentally, and spiritually our sensory receptors for all universal knowledge and understanding are the most efficient. We can tune in clearly. We can communicate clearly. At such times we are on top of the world, believing that we can accomplish anything. We are alert mentally and we feel great physically. We are full of energy, enthusiasm, wisdom, and love. We have opened our direct path.

Our destiny is to navigate our treasure map to find our treasure. Each of us has a treasure. We are presented with many choices, and we come to many forks on the road in our

41

lives. When we choose, we are navigating our treasure map. Those that make enough correct choices find the Kingdom of Heaven on Earth. We have all read about these people. They are the athletes who recognized and nurtured their athletic treasure. They are the doctors and lawyers who recognized and nurtured their intellectual treasure. They are the computer software programmers who work in the countryside communicating by fax or by modem. They are the chefs who prepare their favorite delicacies. They are the restaurateurs who mingle and share with their patrons. They are the forest rangers who maintain the balance in the forest. All have found a special place on this earth where they are contributing to mankind while they are at peace at their best in their chosen environment.

Spirituality is not reserved for preparing for the hereafter in some other life. Spirituality is preparing the Kingdom of God in this life. It is about making the right choice for tomorrow and next week. It is about using our full power to navigate. The beauty of this mechanism is that we are never at a dead end. We can always choose another road, go down another path, pick up another trail. We can always begin again from today. When we use this special mechanism for our treasure hunt, we send questions to our subconscious mind. Our subconscious tunes those special sensory receptors to the universal bank of knowledge. Intuition is fed by a river of energy that is the total sum of all energy. The power we get from the river, the source of energy, is different for every individual. The power is dependent on the health and strength of the sensory receptors in our mind. The health and strength of the sensory receptors is dependent on how successful we have been in shaping our life up until then. If we have made too many wrong choices and if we have too many wrong turns at each intersection on our map, we are farthest afield from that treasure. We must navigate our way back one intersection at a time. The closer we get to the treasure, the stronger the signal becomes. The more correct choices we make, the healthier and clearer are the sensory receptors in our nervous system.

The more knowledge and awareness we have, the closer to the truth we become. The closer to the truth we become, the clearer our perception of what our journey should be, and the better our focus on our role and destiny. When we are close to our pearl we get strong signals and more enlightenment.

Stop some day when you have fifteen or twenty minutes for total relaxation and silence. Sit in a nice comfortable easy chair. Close your eyes and clear your mind. Don't try to concentrate on any one thought. Let all thoughts pass through effortlessly. Enjoy them but do not dwell on them. When you are completely relaxed, pose a question to yourself but don't wait for the answer. Go with the flow. That is one part meditation. Repeat the question three or four times, but then let it pass. Continue to relax for the fifteen to twenty minutes. You may not get an answer in those fifteen to twenty minutes. But be aware that the answer will come at some time and be prepared to recognize it. That is the one part intuition. It will surface at some point, perhaps while you are relaxing, sleeping, or studying. When the answer comes, grasp it and reflect on it. Then reflect on the process that led to the answer. When you have the time, repeat the meditation process once in the morning and once in the evening. As the cobwebs clear from your mind and the receptors and nerve pathways get healthier, the process will become more powerful.

As the spiritual signal gets weaker and weaker for many people today, organized religion is finding it increasingly difficult to lead people properly. As man becomes more knowledgeable, it is impossible to lead through intimidation or fear. Organized religions are, therefore, trying to reach out with more love and understanding. Modern science has played havoc with some of our religious myths. As science reaches into space, probes beneath the sea, reaches back in time, and unlocks genetic codes, beliefs are being unveiled as myths.

Now the churches' focus turns to love, understanding, and compassion. The focus is on removing the limitations on people, rather than placing more limitations on them. As the churches pursue this course, they are discovering that it has a different effect on their church. More and more people are becoming involved in church services and are increasingly moved by the generosity of the clergy. The harsh views of the past are being replaced by peaceful prodding or enlightenment.

Basically, spirituality's prime responsibility is to keep the path between mind, body, and the energy of God open. It is there to help man remove all perversions from mind and body, and to provide stimuli for us to reach deeply into ourselves, to heal ourselves, and to make all mental and physical pathways healthy, vibrant, and conductive. With a healthy pathway of the nervous system or the bloodstream, the daily nourishment of meditation and prayer keeps us growing better and better every day in every way. Any deviation from this role is self-serving. When the role of the church is performed properly it allows all its members to nourish mind, body, and soul.

There are many religions in this world, but most have at their core a Supreme Being. The variations will all change as man's understanding evolves. But there is one constant. We all have a direct connection with God. We need guidance only to the extent that our physical self is out of balance. The more we can balance the nervous system, the better we can clear our mind, and the healthier we make our body, the greater the influx of energy from the universal energy. The only limitation to man is man's acceptance of limitation. There is great abundance in the universe, but we see only limitation. These limitations are man's limitations.

Did you ever notice how getting a great new idea for a product or service is the easy part? You would think that coming up with the idea is the most difficult part. It is usually rises from our intuition with ease. Only when we reveal the idea to someone else does it begin to sound unreasonable. What a mistake it is to discuss it, though we have all done so. Before we leave the discussion, we are convinced we must have been demented to even think of the idea. Even if our family members give us some support, we are soon told by friends why our idea is bad.

Those who succeed don't run to the nearest family member. They sit back and they go back to where the idea came from, their intuition. They start a dialogue with their intuition. They pose questions. Answers come back. Soon they have a complete game plan through which no one can shoot holes. It remains their secret until it is more than a half-baked idea. They proceed when the idea is completely formed and the strength of the package can withstand the pounding from the outside world.

This is one facet of the process of spiritualism. When we get an idea of who we are and what we are and where we are going, it's best to turn inward and pray and to meditate until the strength of our belief is strong enough to withstand the torrent of negative talk that will greet our faith. This is the one private place where we can think out everything clearly until it is ready. We must ask for guidance inwardly. We must ask what is right for us. Then when we get the answer, we must make a positive statement to pursue the result of the answer to its fruition.

The element of spirituality is the simplest of all to use and it is by far the most powerful in shaping our lives. When we achieve results it strikes us with its blend of power and simplicity. Picture a universe which for centuries has remained disciplined and structured and solid. The earth always revolves around the sun as it spins on its axis and it always remains the same distance from all other stars. Think of the power and simplicity of that structure.

No one is ever alone if we can stop, relax, and listen. All the knowledge and truth are available to us if we stop, question and reflect, and question again. It's like the surf of the ocean hitting the sandy beach. It is steady, complete and dependable. We must continually draw from it. The more we solicit the knowledge and truth inwardly, the more truth and knowledge we will uncover. It is no different from the use of physical exercise to bring health, growth, and comfort to our bodies.

It is as though we had two minds. The first mind controls all our conscious thought and propels all our bodily and mental functions. Then there is a second mind that processes all our questions, ideas, and beliefs. This mind contains our self-image. Our self-image is a product of perceiving things in our environment, communicating to our second mind, and forming the view of ourselves that we believe. To change the self-image we can feed in the change we want and that change will be processed.

As we learn to communicate with the second mind, which may be perceived as the subconscious, the answers will become easier and easier. As we cultivate this path we will learn that all the answers are available. All the knowledge and truth can be reached. Meditation and self-talk are the key.

The power of the universe available to drive us is like tying a jumbo jet to a go-cart. Yet, too often, we turn off that power. We try to plug into some human power group. This is like tying the power of a candle to the back of the go-cart.

Early in our lives, we accept spiritual teachings as facts. They are put into practice with all the intellectual capacity we possess at that time. Through our teen years, the noise around us begins to drown out their meaning. The meanings begin to conflict with our social drive for acceptance. They begin to appear contradictory with every other experience around us. We put them in the background. Spirituality needs peace and quiet. We, as teens and young adults, need people and noise.

When we mature and our social life grows more quiet, we again become more attentive to the voice inside us. That's when we begin again, questioning the beliefs and values that have gotten us this far. We begin to develop new beliefs. We form new values. We begin to eliminate some of our myths. The success of the new beliefs and values leads us to continue the treasure hunt.

To reach our full potential, to obtain all the energy and power we need, we must turn inward. Our fuel comes from within. It works as surely as sleep works to power us in our daily activity. If we want to be the most outgoing person in the world, we must turn inward until our self-image is the most exuberant, vibrant, enthusiastic, outgoing person we can imagine. If we want to be a writer, we must turn inward and start writing until the words begin to flow with ease. Whatever the desire, we must turn inward until the answer comes through our intuition. Everyone has a direct line to the universal energy and truth. It is time to clear that line of sludge and debris. It is time to access the full power of the energy holding the universe in a disciplined structure. This is not a philosophical statement of faith. This is a statement of physical and intellectual fact.

Two techniques, taught by many teachers in various forms, involve daily practice to increase the clarity and power of our direct line. The first technique is meditation. The second technique is creative visualization.[1]

While we meditate, the connection to our subconscious grows stronger. This allows us to focus inwardly and open the communication lines to the subconscious and beyond. It is like connecting a cable for the two-way flow of information for fulfillment of all our dreams and desires. It opens a steady flow of energy between our conscious mind, our subconscious mind, and out the other side to the energy flowing in the universe. When we tap into that source of energy nothing is impossible. There are no limitations.

To be most effective, meditation should take place early in the morning when you are fresh and in the evening when it is time to relax. Meditation should last fifteen to twenty minutes. The idea in meditation is to relax completely. Sit in a comfortable chair with your feet touching the floor. Close your eyes. Let your mind float. Do not hold onto any thoughts. Do not try to block out or reject any thoughts that try to enter. Let all thoughts pass through effortlessly. In some forms of meditation a sound or mantra is allowed to enter and pass through the mind periodically. In others, the meditator is encouraged to project images of all thoughts onto a blank screen. Still in another form, the meditator is told to concentrate on the light of a candle. Choose a form of meditation that is comfortable for you.

Creative visualization can be practiced at the end of meditation or it can be practiced several times a day by itself. After we have cleared our mind through meditation, creative visualization strives to create changes in our life that we desire. The basic content of creative visualization are affirmations.

An affirmation is some change to our self-image or to our lifestyle. It should be a positive change for improvement. The affirmation should be written down to increase our focus. The number of possible affirmations is limitless. For instance, you may want to lose weight, going from 170 pounds to be 150 pounds. The affirmation for losing the twenty pounds would be, "I weigh 150 pounds." The affirmation is stated consciously in our mind and an image of a 150 pound person is formed in our mind. The subconscious will then present us with the opportunities necessary to fulfill our desire. We may find, for instance, that our willpower to resist eating is stronger, or that we are not as hungry each day, or that we choose our food with regard to calorie content more wisely.

Creative visualization should be used in privacy and affirmations should be kept private. When we are turning inward for guidance, communication on our own direct line must be private. Revealing our wishes to others will weaken our resolve and reduce our focus. Affirmations should be personal and stated as though accomplished -- I (personal) weigh 150 pounds (accomplished).

Finally, when stating affirmations it is essential for stronger transmission that positive powerful emotions are used. Some of the most powerful emotions have to do with love, faith, and enthusiasm. By looking into our personal experiences, we can all bring forth examples of these emotions from our past.

By practicing meditation and creative visualization, we will shape our lives spiritually by strengthening our direct line, by improving our self-image, and by increasing our self-confidence.

CHAPTER 5

OUR PERSONAL TOOLS OF PRODUCTION

When people discuss the need for a good healthy diet, two groups generally form. The first group consists of those who are young, apparently healthy, and energetic. The second group is older, less energetic, and apparently in need of a good diet. The first group can generally eat anything and still feel good. Members of the second group have become aware that to feel good each day, they must watch what they eat. It is always difficult, therefore, to explain to the first group the cumulative long-term effects of the proper diet. Members of the first group, when they eventually pass to the second group, do realize the benefits of a good diet. However, those who recognize the benefits of a good diet while still members of the first group will maximize the benefits and prolong their periods of maximum energy.

To understand the need for a good diet, let's review some of the material in Chapter 2. We are what we eat and we can have a tremendous impact on shaping our lives in a relatively short time if we practice good nutrition.

If we go back to the schematic of the body (Figure 2-1) in Chapter 2, at the center of the schematic is the cell. The three key ingredients that flow through the schematic are oxygen, hormones, and nutrients. The health of the cell is dependent on the quality of the three ingredients. The quality of the nutrients that are provided through the digestive system will determine how well the trillions of cells in the body function. The cumulative effect of all the cells determines whether we function with enthusiasm, energy, and wisdom. The cells that form each system in our bodies will determine the effectiveness of those systems by the nutrients they have with which to work. Well-fed healthy brain cells let us think more clearly. Well-fed healthy cells of the nervous system let

49

us process signals from the brain to all parts of the body more crisply. Well-fed healthy cells of the heart will make the heart pump more powerfully.

Again, it's a matter of changing the perception of our environment from the surface of our body and our material surroundings to an environment with the cell at the center. For us to function at our maximum energy, each cell must function at maximum energy. For each cell to function at maximum energy, the proper nutrients must be provided.

Our immediate goal when we eat is to satisfy a craving for our favorite food or to quiet hunger pangs. Our cells in some part of our minds and body are crying out for nutrition. We eat for two reasons. The psychological reason is to satisfy a craving. The biological reason is to get energy. The two criteria of the foods we select are that they must be tasty and nutritious. Selecting a food to satisfy either one criterion or the other is not sufficient. If we eat and drink properly we not only feel physically healthier, but, feel psychologically great as well.

When we eat an english muffin in the morning with a glass of orange juice, we are satisfying a biological need. When we put strawberry jam on the english muffin, we are satisfying our psychological need. Satisfying the psychological need is relatively easy. Our taste buds and years of practice have weeded out those foods that are offensive. Ice cream, candy, or soda satisfy our psychological need. And that need should not be overlooked. But generally, those foods that satisfy only a psychological need require our bodies to expend energy to offset their biological effects. These foods do not provide any nutritional benefit and do not add to our store of protein and hormones used to process our food.

When we eat for nutrition as well as for taste, we consider the total positive or negative effect on our system. Knowing what to eat, for most people, is something learned from trial and error over many years. We all get to know what foods are best for us, what food makes us fat, what food is difficult for us to digest. The difficult part is the implementation. The psychological need is so strong that it so often rules over the biological need, which is more subtle and long-term in nature.

To reach the proper balance in our diet, we must consider not only psychological and biological factors, but also their short-term and long-term effects. In the short-term, we are looking for energy and stamina. In the long-term, we are trying to prevent deterioration of our processing system. The more efficient the processing system, the better the quality of the nutrients introduced in our system, the healthier the cells from the high quality nutrients, and the longer life span of the cells. This translates into a longer life span for all cells and, therefore, for our minds and bodies.

The foods that provide us with best short-term energy boost are not necessarily the kindest to our system in the long term. For instance, to get maximum energy and strength, football players often eat a diet full of high protein red meat. Red meat over the long term requires more from our reserves and our processing system and therefore has a long-term negative effect on our system.

We may reach for a candy bar for a quick energy boost and for a psychological boost. But that candy bar requires that the liver generates more insulin to counteract the sugar.

To consider the short-term and long-term effect, let's look at the biological need for nutrition. As written previously, the cell is at the center of our environment. Each cell must be provided with nutrients. The total effect is to maintain a stable internal environment. The human body produces 100,000 different types of protein. Each has a role to play in the operation and health of our system. The structure of each protein the body must produce is determined by each person's own DNA code. The cells in turn reside in the extracellular fluid which is designed to provide an optimum environment for the cells.

We are responsible for maintaining a sound environment for the cells to maximize energy output. The nervous system keeps score of how well we are doing and issues prompts to get us to add the nutrients to maintain or modify our internal environment. For instance, through the hypothalamus gland in the brain, the nervous system prompts you to eat and drink when required. When you become thirsty, this gland issues a prompt to replace the water you are losing through sweat or digestion.

There are five basic steps to providing a healthy diet. These are:

1. Become knowledgeable about the nutrients provided by each food.

2. Determine the amount of energy (calories) for weight loss or gain.

3. Substitute foods that provide energy in the proper ratio of carbohydrates/ proteins/fats.

4. Eat foods rich in fiber, beta-carotene, and potassium.

5. Drink plenty of water.

To become knowledgeable about the nutritional value of various foods, a guide is required. Several good brochures are available for a nominal fee from the U.S. Consumer Information Center. Nutritive Value of Foods (approximately $2.75) and Calories and Weight Pocket Guide (approximately $1.75) are two of the best. For a free consumer information catalog, write to: Consumer Information Center, P.O. Box 100, Pueblo, Colorado 81002.

The Nutritive Value of Foods manual lists the nutritional value of 908 foods. It also contains a table on the Recommended Daily Dietary Allowances (RDA). Typical foods are shown in Table 5-1.

Also included in the manual are values for phosphorous, iron, vitamin A, thiamin, riboflavin, niacin, and ascorbic acid. A typical entry for the Recommended Daily Dietary Allowances states that a male person between the ages of 19 to 22 being 5' 10" tall and weighing 154 pounds should consume 2,900 calories per day for maintenance of weight and health.

If we examine the three food entries in Table 5-1, there are several items of significance: (1) The first item of significance is the calorie content: banana-105, cheeseburger-300, carrot-30. These values when added together determine the total amount of energy we take in each day. Energy is measured in calories. (2) The second significant item is the relative ratios of carbohydrates/protein/fat: banana-27/1/1, cheeseburger-28/15/15, carrot- 7/1/Tr (Tr for Trace). To provide maximum efficiency, our diet should contain for each day a percentage ratio of 55%/15%/30% for carbohydrate/protein/fat.

The relative percentage for these three are: banana-93%/3.5%/3.5%, cheeseburger-48%/26%/26%, carrot-88%/12%/0. (3) A third significant item is the amount of cholesterol: banana-0, cheeseburger-44, carrot-0. (4) A fourth significant item is the ratio of potassium to sodium: banana-98%/2%, cheeseburger-25%/75%, carrot-90%/10%. In each case, the ratios for a healthy diet favor the banana and carrot over the cheeseburger.

Once we become knowledgeable about the nutritional value and calorie content of food, we can begin to modify our diet by substituting foods with better nutritional value and lower calorie content. This modification should not be a test of will, but rather a realignment of eating habits to be used for life. This should not be a lose quick/gain back quick weight loss scheme. The period of adjustment may take one, two, or more years. But day by day, the modification will improve our mental and physical health.

Table 5-1

	Grams	Water Percent	Food Energy Calories	Protein Grams	Fat Grams	Saturated Grams	Fatty Acids Mono- unsaturated Grams	Poly- unsaturated Grams
1 Banana	114	74	105	1	1	0.2	Trace	0.1
1 Cheeseburger	112	46	300	15	15	7.3	5.6	1.0
1 Carrot	72	88	30	1	Trace	Trace	Trace	0.1

	Cholesterol Miligrams	Carbohydrates Grams	Calcium Miligrams	Potassium Miligrams	Sodium Miligrams
1 Banana	0	27	23	451	1
1 Cheeseburger	44	28	135	219	672
1 Carrot	0	7	19	233	25

The first step in the formulation of new habits is to sit down and list the food you currently eat in your diet. Next list the calories for each food from the guide and add up the total number of calories. To maintain your weight, your diet should contain a certain amount of calories. There are many charts that contain weight and calorie data. To adjust your weight up or down, you need to adjust the amount of calories up or down. To reduce weight by one pound, a person must reduce the calorie intake by 3000 calories[1]. To lose five pounds requires the reduction of approximately 3000 x 5 or 15,000 calories. To calculate the amount of weight loss or weight gain over a desired period of time multiply 3000 by the number of pounds to lose or gain and divide by the number of days in the desired period. For instance, to lose ten pounds in thirty days requires that the diet be reduced by 1000 calories each day (3000 calories/pound x 10 pounds ÷ 30 days). If the normal calorie intake is 2900, the daily diet would be reduced to 1900 calories per day for thirty days.

The next chapter, Exercise, contains a discussion of weight gain or loss based on calorie gain or loss through a combination of exercise and nutrition. For the time being, just remember one pound = 3000 calories.

To lose 1 pound in one week, dividing 3000 calories by seven days, you would have to reduce your current diet by approximately 425 calories per day for seven straight days. That would mean cutting out one piece of pie or five cookies per day for seven days. To lose 10 pounds, continue that diet adjustment for ten weeks.

The second critical step in modifying our diet is to substitute foods with a desirable balance of carbohydrates to proteins to fats.

The proper combinations of food or percentage of calories that you eat each day should contain no less than 55% carbohydrates, 15% protein, and less than 30% fat. These are the percentages recommended by the National Research Council, a branch of the National Academy of Science.

If you are a twenty-two year old woman weighing 120 pounds, your calorie intake should be 2100 calories. To reach the balanced action of C/P/F of 55/15/30% your daily diet would contain approximately 1155 calories of carbohydrates, 315 calories of protein, and less than 630 calories of fat. To reach optimum levels, carbohydrates would be increased further and fats would be reduced more drastically. Excellent sources for the 55% of carbohydrates are fruits, vegetables, breads and cereals, grains, peas and beans, pastas such as macaroni and spaghetti, nuts and seeds.

To begin substituting foods, review the list of the foods you normally eat. List by breakfast, lunch, dinner, and snacks. From the manual Nutritive Value of Foods, or from other books containing similar data, write next to each food the amount of calories, proteins, carbohydrates, and fat. In fact, consider preparing a form similar to Figure 5-1 with food down the left margin and the four groups as headings.

Total the calories for each meal and for the full day. Then calculate the percentages of carbohydrates, proteins, and fats. If the percentages are close to or better than 55/15/30, you have a healthy diet. If the ratios are lower than 55% of carbohydrates, you must begin to substitute healthier foods. Look through your Nutritive Value of Foods manual and find substitutes that are higher in carbohydrates and that appeal to your sense of taste. Enter these in the form where it will be used as a substitute and recalculate the percentages.

Figure 5-1

Nutrition Value Calculation										
Weight:_____ Calories per day:_____ Date:___/___/___										
Food		Calories		Carbo.		Protein		Fat		Substitute Food
Breakfast	Sub		Sub		Sub		Sub		Sub	
Total										
Lunch										
Total										
Dinner										
Total										
Snacks										
Total for day										
Percent										

As you begin to substitute in your diet to attain the proper ratio of C/P/F, also seek out foods rich in fiber, beta-carotene, and potassium. The fiber reduces cholesterol. Beta-carotene removes toxic substances and, evidence suggests, it prevents some forms of cancer. Potassium balances the sodium to maintain a balanced nervous system.

Cholesterol is needed by the cells to produce hormones. It is the excess over what is used that causes the bloodstream to clog up and produce atherosclerosis. Cholesterol is manufactured by the liver and transported via the blood stream for the cells to use. It is synthesized from scratch from inside the cells. Protein receptors pull cholesterol inside the cell to produce hormones, the cell membrane, Vitamin D, and other products.

In addition to being manufactured by the body, cholesterol is consumed in the foods we eat. The challenge is to keep cholesterol below 200. The best solution known today is to eat soluble fiber. Many people are aware of the success of eating oat brans and beans, both high in fiber, to reduce cholesterol. The reason soluble fiber works is that digestive fluid of output bile has to be manufactured to process the fiber.[2] This digestive fluid uses cholesterol. The more cholesterol used by the liver to process the fiber, the less cholesterol available to circulate in the bloodstream. Foods rich in fiber include: whole-grain breads, whole-grain cereals, legumes (kidney beans, lima beans, navy beans, split peas), fruits (skins and edible seeds), nuts, and seeds.[3]

Foods rich in beta-carotene reduce the toxic substances in our system. This toxic material harms the cells and reduces their life-span. Foods rich in beta-carotene include:

Vegetables	Fruits
Spinach	Cantaloupe
Sweet potatoes	Mango
Carrots	Papaya
Butternut &	Apricots
hubbard squash	Nectarines
Collard greens	Peaches
Dandelion greens	
Kale	
Turnip greens	
Beet greens	
Red peppers	
Swiss chard	
Bok choy	
Mustard greens	
Tomatoes	
Broccoli	

Potassium needs special mention for a healthy diet because so many of our foods contain salt and a balance between the two is necessary for a healthy nervous system. Generally the key to a good balance for potassium and sodium is to include several servings of fruits and vegetables in the daily diet. Foods rich in potassium include: milk, apricots, bananas, dates, figs, juices, oranges, peaches, prunes, walnuts, watermelon, dry beans, dry peas, broccoli, brussels sprouts, carrots, cauliflower, potatoes, pumpkin, and squash. Most fruits and vegetables are high in potassium and low in sodium. Fruits in particular have a high potassium, low sodium content.

Finally, to keep all systems functioning properly, it is necessary to drink plenty of water each day. The daily recommended total is eight glasses per day. In an article by Dr. Donald Robertson in <u>McCalls</u>, January, 1986, the following quotation appeared. "Incredible as it may seem, water is quite possibly the single most important catalyst in losing weight and keeping it off. Although most of us take it for granted, water may be the only true 'magic potion' for permanent weight loss." As Dr. Robertson states, drinking water suppresses the appetite and helps the body metabolize stored fat. He points to five benefits when the body gets sufficient water: endocrine gland function improves, fluid retention is alleviated, more stored fat is used as fuel, natural thirst returns, and there is loss of hunger.

To summarize for a healthy diet, complete the following steps:

1. Become knowledgeable about nutrients provided by each food.

2. Determine the amount of energy (calories) for weight loss or gain.

3. .Substitute foods that provide energy in the proper ratio of carbohydrate/protein/fat.

4. Eat foods rich in fiber, beta-carotene, and potassium.

5. Drink plenty of water.

CHAPTER 6

EXERCISING FOR ENERGY

When it comes to exercise, our society is divided into two groups. The first contains people who are compelled to exercise and who recognize and need the psychological, biological, and physical boost that exercise provides. The second group is made up of people who rarely exercise, who do not see any value or need to exercise, and do not have the discipline to conduct a regular exercise program.

For those in Group 1, many books have been written that provide detail on every calisthenic, isotonic, and aerobic. The readers understand the benefits of exercise. If this chapter were only more detail about the techniques of exercise, it would be as the cliché states, "preaching to the choir." This chapter, therefore, is presented as an option for people in Group 2. What is it in our makeup that can make exercise seem like such a chore? Why is it so tough psychologically to get going? Everyone seems to agree on the benefits. Everyone loves the results. Getting started is truly a case of mind over matter. The mind must be motivated to move the body to dislodge the matter that is clogging up our bloodstream and our cells. The cells must be freed to produce energy.

People know that calisthenics, aerobics, and other exercise have a beneficial cumulative effect. But the results are slow in arriving. The change in physical stature is sure but slow. Discipline is necessary. When the discipline is developed, and the exercise starts, there is a great deal of inertia to overcome. But as momentum grows, a switch in our mind trips and the exercise changes from chore to challenge. At times, as exuberance grows, overextension becomes a concern. But at some point the exercise gives a large psychological, biological, and physical boost.

This boost comes because we begin to take in more oxygen, our muscles loosen and become more flexible and stronger, the heartbeat accelerates, hormones are released, nutrients accelerate through the bloodstream, and cells begin to generate energy. Lethargy begins to disappear. Waste is expelled from the cells and carried out through the bloodstream more rapidly. Sweat flows out of pores. Fat begins to dissolve. We seem to get a lighter, cleaner feeling. Our body is more relaxed and our mind is more alert. We become exhilarated. We become happy with ourselves. Anxiety disappears. We get a good, relaxed, tired feeling.

To be most effective, exercise should be considered an extension of the weight control program started for nutrition. If we go back to the example in Chapter 5 for losing 1000 calories per day, we can, by adding exercise to the equation, make it easier to lose weight. Instead of having to reduce our diet by 1000 calories, we can reduce our diet by 500 calories and increase our activity to burn 500 calories. Losing 500 calories by exercise would require gardening for one hour or jogging/walking for forty-five minutes. If our stamina and endurance are at a high level, all 1000 calories can be burned off by exercise. But a balance between diet and exercise is best[1]. To state this in equation form:

Weight Loss Calories = Nutrition Calories + Exercise Calories

1000 Calories (1/3 pounds/day) = N 500 Calories + E 500 Calories

Beginners often make a major mistake when they get the urge to get in shape. They start too quickly. Before they can achieve the results they want, they become discouraged by the rigor. Many exercisers, for instance, start with a running program. After a week or two, they become discouraged. It is difficult to stay motivated for every run with so few apparent results.

An exercise program should be shaped to start slowly. A good exercise program has two components. The program must build muscular strength and flexibility and it must build cardiovascular endurance. For the muscular strength portion of the program, a novice exerciser, for instance, might start with basketball and walking. As muscular strength improves and to work on cardiovascular endurance, the exerciser can accelerate the walking and add bicycling, or can move to a jogging-walking condition. As strength and endurance increase, swimming or cross-country skiing might be added. The starting activity must be something the novice enjoys doing. The physical activity can be an activity currently part of the exerciser's daily routine.

For a Group 2 or novice exerciser, there are four basic steps for starting the program.

1. Determine the portion of the weight loss to be accomplished through exercise.

2. Determine from Table 6-1 what activity is required to burn off the calories in Step 1.

3. Start building muscular strength and flexibility by using the activities selected in Step 2.

4. Select activities to increase the heartbeat level to build cardiovascular endurance.

The key to a good exercise or to the benefits of an activity not ordinarily listed as an exercise is the oxygen intake during the period of exercise. The term "aerobics" has become synonymous with healthy exercise. The definition of aerobics is "living, active, or occurring only in the presence of oxygen." You recall in Chapter 2 we discussed three things that are provided to the cells to produce energy -- nutrients from the food we eat, hormones from the glands, and air or oxygen through the lungs. Food provides the nutrients. Exercise provides the oxygen. To maximize energy production from the cells, we must maximize the amount and quality of usable nutrients in our food and we must maximize the amount of oxygen in the air we breathe. In his book Aerobics, Kenneth H. Cooper, states that with the proper exercise, "your lungs begin processing more air with less effort, your heart grows stronger, pumping more blood with fewer strokes, the blood supply to your muscles improve, and your total volume increases."[2]

In short, when we exercise, we are improving our body's capacity to bring in oxygen and deliver it to the tissue cells, where it is combined with foodstuffs to produce energy.

For traditional exercise programs, the best all-around exercise to provide muscle strength and flexibility and cardiovascular endurance is cross country skiing. The poling activity of the arms and the kicking and gliding of the legs exercise the shoulders, back, chest, abdomen, buttocks, and legs. With mechanical cross-country ski machines now available, the benefits of this super exercise can be enjoyed year round. Other excellent aerobic exercises are jogging, swimming, and bicycling.

But, as stated earlier, the primary purpose of this chapter is not to help a Group 1 person grow stronger and healthier. It is to help Group 2 individuals to improve their health to the point where they can approach the starting line to a more vigorous, enthusiastic lifestyle.

The objective of the exercise program is to continue to build on the lessons of the chapter on nutrition. The goal is to integrate physical activity and nutrition. Nutrition and exercise must work together to provide fuels for each cell, to enable the cells to produce energy, and to ensure that all excess fuels and waste are ejected from our system.

Let us go back to Step 1 of our four step program. How many calories per day, above our normal activity, must we expend to achieve our desired weight? For best results consider doing exercise every other day. If exercise is desired each day, alternate between exercise for muscular strength and flexibility and exercise for cardiovascular endurance.

Table 6-1 contains a list of activities. Next to each activity are the calories that it burns in one hour. Once you determine how many calories to burn each day above your normal activity, select activities from this list that will achieve the desired result. If you have a favorite activity that is not on the list, match it to an activity of similar difficulty on the list and use the calories shown as an equivalent.

If, for instance, we want to lose one pound each week, our weekly diet must be reduced by 3000 calories or our weekly exercise must be increased to burn another 3000 calories.

If we look at Table 6-1 for a beginning exercise, we see that walking briskly and cycling are moderate activities. Each burns 460 calories per hour. To burn 3000 calories per week requires 6.5 hours of exercise per week. Exercising every other day would require approximately 2 hours of

TABLE 6-1

	Calories Expended Per Hour of Exercise	
	Man	Woman
(140Pounds)	(175	Pounds)
Sitting quietly	100	80
Standing quietly	120	95
Light activity: 　Cleaning house 　*Dancing slowly 　Office work 　Playing baseball 　Playing golf	300	240
Moderate activity: 　*Badminion 　*Canoeing 　Cycling 　Dancing fast 　Gardening 　*Mowing 　Playing basketball 　*Skating (ice or roller) 　*Tennis 　*Volleyball 　Walking briskly (3.5 mph)	460	370
Strenuous activity: 　Cross-country skiing 　*Mountain climbing 　Racqeutball 　Running (7 min/mile)	730	580

Source: Dietary Guidelines for Americans
　　　　　Third Edition
　　　　　U.S. Department of Agriculture
　　　　　U.S. Department of Health and Human Services
*(Amended by adding items with asterisk)

walking or cycling each exercise day. To reduce walking or cycling to one hour every other day, diet reduction can be used to reach 3000 calories.

For one hour every other day or 3.5 exercise periods per week, 1,610 calories are burned through walking or cycling (460 x 3.5). To reach a loss of 3,000 calories per week means reducing our diet by 1,390 calories per week (3,000-1,610) or 200 calories per day (1390 ÷ 7 days). Therefore to lose one pound per week would require walking every other day for one hour and giving up three cookies or an english muffin or an order of french fries on each day. To lose ten pounds in ten weeks continue the same regimen. If you begin adjusting your diet from the chapter on nutrition, simply start by adding 3.5 hours of walking or cycling each week.

Set up your own weight control program. Continue to modify your diet by eating the proper ratio of carbohydrates, protein, and fat, and by eating the proper amount of calories. Next calculate the number of calories that your physical activity will expend. Then use both nutrition and exercise to balance the equation until you are able to maintain your weight at the level you prefer. Do not try to jump start your exercise program by doing some activity that is alien to you. Start by increasing the amount of physical activity already in your daily routine. Instead of taking elevators, start walking up the stairs. Instead of using the telephone, start walking to visit the person. Instead of using the clothes chute, start carrying the laundry up and down the stairs. Instead of driving, walk to the drugstore or grocery store. As your fitness improves, your desire for more rigorous workouts will increase. You may even develop the instincts of a Group 1 Exerciser.

At this point we have actually completed steps 1,2, and 3 of our 4 step program. (1) We have determined the number of calories to burn through exercise. (2) We have selected the physical activity to burn the calories. (3) We have begun to build muscular strength and flexibility by using that activity. We even have touched on increasing to a small degree the cardiovascular endurance of step 4.

To complete step 4 and dramatically improve our cardiovascular endurance, we must increase our physical activity to a level that increases our heartbeat rate and keeps it at the higher level for a sufficient amount of time. In most cases, that requires activities above the 500 calorie per hour range. But when you are starting out, lower levels of activity may accelerate the heartbeat rate to the desired level. As you improve, an increase to more strenuous activity is required.

The key to this part of the program is to calculate the target heart rate that is required for your current fitness level. The calculation proceeds as follows:

Subtract your age from 220
Multiply that result by a value of 55% to 85% depending on the following:

Current Condition	Min Rate/ Max Rate
Sedentary	55%/75%
Moderate Exerciser	60%/80%
Group 1 Exerciser	65%/85%

If you were 50 and just starting from a sedentary level, your target heart rate would be:

220 - 50 = 170 x 55% or x 75% = A minimum of 94 and a maximum of 128 beats per minute. For a 200 pound man of various ages and levels of conditioning, the target heart rates would be:

220- Age	Age	Sedentary (55 to 75)
20	300	110-150
30	190	105-143
40	180	99-135
50	170	94-128

220- Age	Age	Moderate (60 to 80)	Group 1 (65 to 85)
20	300 120-160	130-170	
30	190 114-152	124-162	
40	180 108-144	117-153	
50	170 102-136	111-145	

The minimum heart rate must be reached to benefit the cardiovascular system. The maximum heart rate should not be exceeded to ensure that the cardiovascular system is not damaged.

To measure your heart rate, take the finger tips of one hand and place them on your wrist, just below the hand on the thumb side of the hand. Count the pulse for ten seconds and multiply by six or count for twenty seconds and multiply by three. To measure the heart rate accurately, you must measure immediately after you stop exercising because the heart rate decreases rapidly when you stop. There can be a significant change after twenty seconds.

Before you do your aerobics, always stretch and warm up. At the conclusion, slow gradually to allow for a cool down period.

The duration of your activity or exercise will be determined by your heart rate measurement. Five minutes of exercise is better than no exercise. Your goal initially will be to work through to your second wind. There are, generally, two phases in exercise. In the first phase, we tire quickly and then the body generates the reserve energy and we get a second wind. When you feel exhaustion in the first phase, stop and measure your heart rate. If it has not exceeded the maximum, continue to exercise. If it has reached the maximum, stop and rest until the heat rate returns to normal.

To gain the maximum benefits by having the energy production come from stored fat rather than carbohydrates, the exercise period must be at least fifteen minutes long. The frequency of the exercise should be three times a week or every other day. Select your own pace. Start slowly. Build your stamina and lengthen your exercise period. With an integrated nutrition and exercise program, you will begin feeling better day by day.

CHAPTER 7

THE STAIRCASE OF SELF-ESTEEM

Education leads to awareness. Awareness leads to change. Change leads to growth. Growth leads to greater self-confidence, to greater self-esteem, and to maturity. This is the cycle of education.

There are hundreds of facets to our character. Each facet is formed by a belief that we hold to be a fact, the truth. Each time we learn something new or become aware of other facts, the facts we hold as truth become more entrenched or are replaced by new beliefs. When we accept a new belief, a new fact, we change. When we change by getting closer to the truth, we grow. Our self-esteem grows from the realization. Our confidence grows. We become more mature. We are better suited to face the challenges of life.

Getting to the truth is a learning experience a little bit like peeling an onion. The removal of each layer leads us to a more poignant purer part of the same onion, closer to the core. Education peels away the layers in our perceptions that disguise the truth in its absolute form. But at each layer some composite part of the truth exists. Education strips away the layers and peels away untruths and myths.

It we are totally successful, education will lead us to truth in its absolute form. At its absolute, truth puts us in complete harmony with all natural universal law and allows us to draw on the natural universal energy. The practical results in our life are a high level of confidence with high self-esteem, which allows us to be self-sufficient.

Education starts from the first day out of the womb. Everything that we begin to sense and hear and feel begins to form into beliefs that we hold. We hold and rub a blanket and translate that action into a belief about blankets, cloth, softness, and comfort. Our learning increases in degree of sophistication throughout our lives. The more mature, the more aware, the truer our perceptions, the greater our wisdom.

In our early years our perceptions and awareness and, therefore, the majority of the beliefs we hold come from our parents. They are the source of our truths. The ease of our progress is dependent on the maturity of their perceptions. As our personality is formed, our view of reality is colored by our biological and environmental characteristics. The individuality of these traits paints a different view of reality for each of us. The same facts revealed to two people will lead to two different views of the same reality. As we proceed through the stages of pre-school, grammar school, high school, and college we form a myriad of beliefs carved from a myriad of influences. Change and growth are relatively rapid. Our beliefs, having been composed freely and easily from the experience of others, are basically the needs of the majority in society. Our own needs, our inner needs have not, for the most part, been addressed. The opportunity to examine our beliefs in terms of our own needs occurs after our formal education.

Education, through the formal years, is basically education through our five senses. Education, through our adult years, begins to add elements of intellect and intuition.

When we pass into our mid-twenties it is usually a time to begin again. Adulthood provides greater freedom to peel more layers away, to increase awareness in areas previously closed.

Awareness is defined by Dr. Robert Anthony in the following manner, "Your awareness can be defined as the clarity with which you consciously and unconsciously perceive and understand everything that affects your life. It is the sum total of your experiences encompassing conditioning, knowledge, intellect, intuition, instinct, and all that you perceive through the five senses. Your present level of awareness indicates your moods, attitudes, emotional reactions, prejudices, habits, desires, anxieties, fears, aspirations and goals."[1]

The challenge in education is to take the courses that will provide us with the opportunity to evaluate our current perceptions in the light of new facts, new truths from a new social setting in a new environment. Truths can stand the test

70

only if they hold firm across several environments. Once such a truth stands the test, it becomes a rock in our foundation.

When awareness increases in any direction, a change will take place. The change can be very subtle. A new bit of information stored in the mind is as much a change as a new bit of data entered into computer memory. Decisions based on the group of facts with which that bit is a part will be modified because of that new bit.

Everyone, therefore, depending on their exposure to new facts, is going through change on a consistent basis. When NASA shoots a spacecraft to photograph the moon, the new awareness of the moon changes the data base of information about the universe and the new information affects our thinking and decisions about future space exploration.

Change is exciting to some and threatening to others. Many see change as an expansion of their knowledge and information and as an opportunity to reevaluate the truths they hold. Others see change as a threat and an intrusion to their beliefs. But both groups eventually accept change as new truth and must use the data in their decision process. Eventually it becomes an impression on the mind, a part of the total memory bank. Good data leads to sound decisions. Bad data leads to poor decisions.

Change can result from data received from any of the twelve ways in which our lives are shaped. A study on the effects of eating a piece of chocolate cake may lead to a change in eating habits. New data on the effects of doing sit-ups may lead to a change in exercise habits. An oil crisis may cause a change in the school calendar, which causes a change in student study habits. The purchase of a summer cottage changes the buyer's perception of freedom.

At one time or another we all search to change one facet or another of our lives. One may search for knowledge to overcome an allergy, or search for knowledge to improve one's sleep, or search for a new career opportunity. With every search comes an increase in awareness. With an increase in awareness comes change in beliefs and in behavior.

When an increase in awareness leads to a positive change, the purpose of education is satisfied. When a person grows and matures, the quality of life improves for that person and for all the people around. We grow and we are able to peel away the facade. More of the real person is allowed to surface.

Growth occurs rapidly from birth through the teen years. We learn rapidly in an intense educational setting through twelve to sixteen years of school. The curriculum is a blend of communicative skills, vocational skills, and cultural skills. For each the lessons of society are drawn. The ultimate goal should be to create confident, self-reliant people with high self-esteem.

At a minimum education provides the ability to communicate in a particular culture. The minimum is the standard reading, writing, and arithmetic. How far a person progresses beyond those basics determines the quality of life. The very minimum accepted today, in our culture, for a degree of dignity and quality is a high school education. A high school education with the proper blend of communicative skills and vocational skills is the basic requirement. But to function in a full and fluent manner in this society, an individual must blend communicative, vocational, and cultural skills in the formal educational curriculum. This preparation leads to an awareness that considers not only the needs of society but also considers the biological, environmental, and psychological needs of the individual.

At a minimum, education provides job related training, which allows operation of the machines of industry. Operation implies the ability to work functionally with the machinery and to communicate in the industrial language used within an industry. Courses in math and science are provided to prepare students to communicate and to operate. The division of labor requires only a portion of the curriculum for operation. But the remainder provides for communication within all divisions of labor.

When an education in cultural skills is added, communication skills increase beyond the basic functionality of industry and provide an awareness in the psychological needs and aptitudes of that industry. Those aware of three skills--communication, vocational, and cultural--become the managers of the system.

John Dewey in his book <u>Democracy and Education</u>, said, "Since life means growth, a living creature lives as truly and positively at one stage as at another, with the same intrinsic fullness and the same absolute claims. Hence, education means the enterprise of supplying the conditions which ensure growth or adequacy of life irrespective of age." He goes on to say, "Since growth is the characteristic of life, education is all one with growing; it has no end beyond itself."[2]

As we advance up the steps of education, our teachings go from practical to abstract, from social to personal, from physical to intellectual to instinctive to intuitive. Each step brings more awareness, which leads to change and growth. With growth comes confidence and self-esteem. Self-esteem leads to self-sufficiency and independence.

How can we translate these words into steps? First let us look at the steps of education that appear in Figure 7-1.

What do we see when we look at the diagram? The most vivid section of the diagram is the block designated as Basic. These are the earliest steps in our formal education and for most people they are the steps of formal education. From the basic education we should develop the communication, vocational, and cultural skills needed to survive in society. The first educational lessons we receive are in communication. This comes in the form of reading, writing, and arithmetic. With the basic communication skills we can conduct transactions on the playground or in the candy story. The early educational lessons are all social in content. That is all students have the same curriculum. Sometime during the high school years, students begin to personalize their curriculum. This personalization usually is an introduction into basic vocational skills. Students begin to plan for a career in their chosen occupation.

Cultural skills are taught beginning in the later years of grammar school, in some form of history and geography. Through history or geography we learn about the accomplishments of our ancestors and we learn about our neighbors. We become aware of the responsibilities of each generation in maintaining the continuity and continuing the growth of our culture. When we have completed our basic education, we should be prepared to communicate fluently in all exchanges required by our diverse activities. We should be prepared to earn a living through our vocational skills. We should be prepared to understand and communicate with people of diverse cultures and values.

Figure 7-1

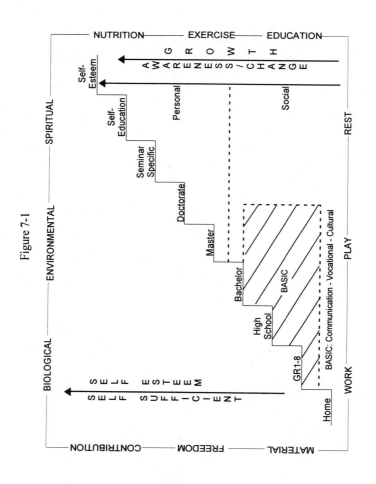

Each step of our education raises our awareness, which leads to change, which leads to growth. As we grow, our self-esteem grows and we become more self-sufficient in every facet of life.

At some point education becomes completely personal. We begin to address the urgings from within that deal with our destiny. We begin to address the urgings from within that ask who are we and what do we want to do. The search through education takes many forms. It can be in the form of individual research or it can come from the support of a larger peer group. Peer support groups in our culture include religious organizations, social clubs, and work related organizations.

In our search for answers people select from a large variety of courses. However, each can be categorized into one of the twelve ways we shape our lives. They all in their own way help us determine who we are and what we do. Each course taken or each seminar attended or research completed fills in some of the blanks that define who we are and what we do. Each educational block is like a letter in our own crossword puzzle that eventually reveals our identity. The more blanks that are filled, the clearer the picture called destiny. Whatever the journey, the ultimate goal of education is the same. That goal is self-esteem. Self-esteem that fills us with joy and well-being while we comfort, prod, and teach others who are still on their journey. Only the person making the journey can determine the level of self-esteem. Only the person making the journey can identify every blank that must still be filled.

Awareness, change, and growth are the great gifts of education. Self-esteem is the reward. The potential of education, formal or informal, social or personal, to shape our lives is unlimited. We need only to choose wisely from the cornucopia. Begin to shape your life through education. Now that you have taken everything thrown at you during your formal training years, it's time to become more personal in your selections. Select one of the twelve components in which you have a strong instinctive interest. Analyze that area and develop it.

If you start with biology, learn about the effect of your thoughts and actions on your anatomy and physiology. If you want to include more spontaneity in your life, learn of the many ways you can add play to your life. The educational choices are unlimited. Answer those urgings through education.

CHAPTER 8

RELEASING PHYSICAL AND MENTAL

STRESS

To know how to rest is more important today than at any other time in civilization. To rest and relax properly is as necessary as exercise. Each takes our mind and body to either end of our cardiovascular spectrum. Exercise makes our heart reach its maximum potential by exerting and building. Rest reaches the very depths of peacefulness and quiet with minimum effort for the heart. This sets us up to live our lives with confidence within that spectrum. If you rest properly, the effects of stress and anxiety are healed as you meditate or sleep.

Rest can take many forms. It is that brief twenty seconds when you push back from everything and take a deep breath. It is that minute or two pause to look at a painting of a beautiful landscape or a serene harbor. It is that twenty minutes when we sit and meditate and allow our minds to relax. It is the hour or two of sitting in our favorite easy chair and reading an inspiring book or watching a good program on television. It is that eight hours of peaceful sleep every night. It is that two weeks vacation during those lazy summer days or that week in the mountains filled with stirring winter days. Each day, each hour we must have a means to sit back and separate ourselves from our daily tasks and relax. The rest periods allow the energy factory the opportunity to catch up.

How we relax during the day sets up the effectiveness of our sleep at night. How do we sleep at night? What is the process of sleep? We do not know that much about the workings of the sleeping mind. Since we are in sleep, we could not consciously make changes in its effectiveness in any case. Our input to sleep occurs before we try to sleep. How rested our mind is at sleep determines the quality of sleep. How stress free our mind is at sleep determines the quality of sleep. We cannot behave in an agitated manner all day and expect to sleep in a relaxed manner all night.

Sleep itself is still such a mystery that Phil Donahue in his book The Human Animal talks about a "Factor S." He writes of scientist who hypothesize that sleep is induced by a build up of chemicals during the day. They call the chemicals "Factor S."[1] Factor S would be similar to a computer register that accumulates a count steadily each day until it hits overflow and is reset after it shuts off all processing.

What is known about sleep is that there are four stages. From light dozing in Stage 1, we proceed to deeper sleep in Stage 2, 3, and 4. From Stage 4 we proceed back through 3 to 2. Stage 2, called REM for rapid-eye-movement, is the stage in which dreaming occurs. One complete cycle from 1 to 4 and back to 2 takes approximately ninety minutes. During each night the average sleeper moves through three or four cycles.

Whether we have dreams or nightmares during the REM stage is determined by the stress level of our mind at bedtime.

Eating and drinking habits, daytime rest habits, exercise habits, and behavior habits all affect the way we sleep.

In her book on sleep, Dianne Hales puts it this way:

"A sleep problem is not 'in your head,' or for that matter, in your body -- but in both. Sleep reflects how you feel, physically and emotionally. Your sleep may be more sensitive to problems of mind or body than your waking consciousness. Throughout the day you may cope marvelously with the challenges and stresses of life. You carry on despite a headache or pulled muscle, frustration, or sadness. Yet however competent you are by day, you can't rely on the same coping skills by night. The signals of mind and body about minor pains or unspoken fears can be ignored during the day, but at night they insist on acknowledgement."[2]

We have all become aware of the effects of caffeine for instance on our ability to function during the day or to sleep at night. We use coffee to wake us up in the morning. Students use coffee or other drinks high in caffeine to keep themselves awake at night. Many people will stop drinking coffee by noon because they are aware of the effect of caffeine on their sleep that night. A heavy meal late at night can affect our sleep. The work of the digestive system may offset the attempt to shut off the body's mechanisms as we try to go to sleep. Alcohol has a considerable effect on the amount of sleep and on the deepness of sleep. It somehow alters the sleep-inducing apparatus especially after two or three hours of sleep and keeps the mind closer to the conscious surface. Other foods and drinks may have a similar, though more subtle affect on our sleep. Long naps during the day can effect the way we sleep at night. It may make it difficult to fall asleep at the usual hour though the hour for rising in the morning remains the same. Exercise late at night may affect the way we sleep.

Basically the success we have in falling asleep and in sleeping peacefully through the night is related to the amount of stress or anxiety that we bring to bed. The stress or anxiety may be induced by food, drink, work, and a myriad of other problems or concerns. The key to a good night's sleep is to minimize the stress and anxiety during the day by applying relaxation techniques during the day. There are generally two elements to a tired condition. There is the expenditure of all energy generated by the cell factory and there is the stress and anxiety of unresolved issues. The first is responsive to rest in normal biological terms. Muscles grow tired and feel weak. We rest. The body shuts down. The muscles are dormant. They are reinvigorated by a good night's sleep. If stress and anxiety were not involved, the work and rest cycle would be steady and predictable.

Did you ever spend a day on the beach or in the mountain air, do nothing, and yet become as sleepy as though you had worked for eight hours. The biological clock continues to operate whatever our activity. Richard M. Coleman in his book states that the human biological clock if left on its own without schedules operates on a twenty-five hour day.[3] The tendency is to get tired one hour later each night from the previous night and sleeping one hour later each morning. We reset the clock by rising at the same hour each morning.

One of the keys to beneficial rest, therefore, is to relax the mind, to clean the mind before we go to bed. Rather than wait, however, until ten minutes before going to bed, we should have methods to free the mind of stress and anxiety throughout the day. We should develop a regimen for rest that is as instinctive as the regimen we have developed for work or play. Our regimen for rest should include twenty second relaxation exercises, one or two minute relaxation exercises, twenty minute relaxation exercises, two hour relaxation exercises, and exercises that will promote eight peaceful hours of sleep.

Did you ever spend the day puttering around the house doing chores? Chances are you slept very well that night. I can recall spending one day each spring just cleaning brush after the winter snows had melted away. I would start a fire. I would cut large limbs requiring the use of a chain saw and I would drag them to the fire. Food and drink was enjoyed during breaks around the fire. At the end of day, my muscles were sore and my energy was low. But sleep that night was as peaceful as it gets. It was peaceful because tiredness from the day's work contained only one element, expenditure of energy. There were no distractions during the day. In fact there was plenty of time for contemplation and introspection. The element of stress and anxiety was completely eliminated. That should be our goal each day. To accomplish that goal we must alternate periods of rest with other activities during the day. The day should end with a good physically tired feeling but with a mind well rested. During the night the mind will continue to work for you, but the body will have its chance to turn off.

One of the benefits of sleep is in allowing the subconscious mind some time to solve problems and to answer questions while the conscious mind hovers in idle. Many people are able to concentrate on a question before sleep and wake up during the night or in the morning with the answer fresh in their mind.

The goal of our daily relaxation regimen should be to end each day with a good pleasant tired feeling free of stress and anxiety. You will recognize this feeling because you will look forward to going to sleep knowing you will sleep peacefully and wake rested and ready to go on to another beautiful day.

RELEASING PHYSICAL AND MENTAL STRESS

What kind of regimen can you develop? Here are some suggestions for relaxing each day as you proceed through your daily routine.

20 second relaxation   -   Breathe deeply
Think pleasant thoughts or
    affirmations
Reflect on a wall painting or
    photograph

2 minute relaxation   -   Reflect on a wall painting or
    photograph
Project yourself to your
    favorite setting and dream
Practice positive affirmations

20 minute relaxation   -   Practice meditation
Do yoga
Practice positive affirmations

2 hour relaxation   -   Read a good book
Walk
Garden
Cut brush
Do aerobics
Bicycle
Golf
Ski
Engage in your favorite
    hobby

The key to a successful regimen is to develop a number of positive affirmations that you can repeat throughout the day. If you have developed the practice of creative visualization from earlier chapters, then these are in place and you can refer to them several times each hour and many times throughout the day. If you have not, this is the time to start. To sit back several times each hour and introduce positives consciously into your mind diffuses the stress that is trying to build up, reminds you of the positive in your life, and keeps the relative importance of each task in focus. If you lean back in your chair for twenty seconds three or four times each hour and take a deep breath, you will relieve much tension. If you sit back take a deep breath and concentrate on a positive affirmation you will relieve tension and refresh your mind. If you lean back take a deep breath and say, "I am completely relaxed," your subconscious mind will signal your conscious mind to relax all muscles.

Once each hour, you should then sit back, release all work tools, take a deep breath and repeat all the affirmations that you are currently using for building the mind. For instance you might sit back, close your eyes, take a deep breath, and repeat four or five affirmations with concentrations and conviction. These might include some of the following:

I am relaxed. I have plenty of time for everything.
I am confident in what I am doing.
Every day in every way I'm getting better and better.
I am the master of my life.
I feel happy and blissful just being alive.
I am vibrantly healthy and radiantly beautiful.
I love to love and be loved.
The more I have the more I have to give.

The third element to relaxation during your daily routine is to find a twenty-minute period once or twice each day for meditation. The most effective times for meditation are once early in the morning to set up your day and once after work hours and before dinner. The meditation should be in a quiet place. You may sit in your favorite easy chair or lie on your bed. Your goal is to relax completely and to let all thoughts pass through your mind effortlessly. There should be no attempt to introduce a thought or to hold a thought. All thoughts should enter and pass freely.

Many books discuss techniques of meditation. Find and use the form and format that put you at ease most effectively. But if there is a delay prior to the completion of your research, begin simply by sitting and relaxing with a deep breath and repeat your affirmations. As you grow more relaxed, do not try to hold any affirmations but rather let them come and go and pass through the mind effortlessly. The positive affirmations always provide a relaxing, cleansing affect. The primary purpose of the meditation is to turn inward, to communicate and connect with your subconscious, and beyond while you leave all your cares from the outside world.

To complete your daily relaxation regimen, spend two hours doing something you enjoy most. Read a good book. Take a bike ride. Clean the weeds in your flower garden. If it is more physical than mental, practice your affirmations as you relax.

If you can relax for twenty seconds or one or two minutes every hour, twenty minutes every morning and night, and two hours every evening, your day will have been spent building and refreshing and you will finish the day with a good tired feeling. Your day's chores will tire you physically, but you will build intellectually.

However, if you should reach the end of the day and there is some element of stress and anxiety remaining, there are several ways in which you can relax and go to sleep.

One of the ways to eliminate stress and anxiety before bedtime is to drink a glass of warm milk. Warm milk produces a natural tranquilizer called L-Trytophane. Drink a coffee mug size cup of warm milk and you will sleep better.

Have you ever noticed that you sleep better in summer when the fan or air conditioning is running or you sleep better in winter when there is a steady hum from the cold-mist humidifier? This is known as the phenomenon of the white noise.

In her book Dianne Hales writes that white noise is a sound involving all frequencies audible to the human ear. It lulls the mind because there is no message in the medium. The frequency is less important than the repetition. Hales states that a form of white noise preferred by many is tape recordings or phonograph records of natural sounds such as waterfalls or birds or the surf hitting the beach.[4]

In his book Coleman talks of keeping a cognitive diary to help you sleep better. He suggests setting aside a twenty-minute period after dinner when you try to worry as much as you can. You write the worries in your diary along with short-term and long-term solutions.[5]

Of course it is worth repeating that anything that stimulates the mind and body, from stirring conversation to exercise to alcohol and caffeine should be avoided before bedtime.

Another effective way to fall asleep is to clean your mind except for one thought. Think of the one thing that makes you most happy and focus on that one thought. Continue to expand on that thought, thinking for example, of how, if you had the opportunity, you would revel in that environment. Let your mind go. Start moving with that scene to more ideal places. Let your mind travel to your vacation spot or sit on a beach or fly to a tropical island. Enjoy. Imagine that your desires are granted as you go. If you fall asleep along your journey so much the better. You will sleep while your subconscious continues to work on your affirmations.

Rest is as important as exercise to our well-being. Begin to develop routines for rest that are sprinkled throughout your day. These restful routines will set up the effectiveness of your eight hours of sleep. Remember to rest for twenty seconds, two minutes, twenty minutes, and two hour periods each day.

CHAPTER 9

REACHING MATURITY IN THE

WORKPLACE

The workplace should have the same ambience, the same joy, the same happiness as all other places in our lives. The workplace should be a place where people come together to apply their unique and individual talents for the successful accomplishment of a project. From the success of that project, each contributor should share in proportion to his giving. Those who are willing to give more should receive more. This utopian view is not yet within our reach due to competition and manipulation.

Currently, in our history the corporation is in its early infancy, far from maturity. Those who provide the investment capital gain the major share of the rewards. Those who provide the labor gain compensation for that labor only. Because investors buy the tools of production-working capital, plant, equipment, and labor, they control the tools of production. An employee has only one of the four tools of production -- labor, and receives compensation for that labor.

The goal of anyone entering the workplace should be to convert the gains of his labor into ownership of the tools of production. The goal should be to become an investor. Then an employee can share in the full responsibility for running that corporation. Each worker reaching that plateau comes much closer to achieving that utopian view.

The confrontation that has changed the workplace from all other places in our lives is that contention over who should share that portion of the burden and who should share that portion of the reward. The contention will be eliminated when the corporate structure matures from a pyramid structure to a network.

Pyramiding which deals with only the exchange of money from one layer to the next is outlawed in most societies because it gives an unfair portion of the rewards to the founder of the pyramid. Those investing at the end of the pyramid life cycle have few investors to approach, after a considerable investment of their own. In the corporate structure that is currently preferred, the founder adds new layers to the pyramid as the business grows. The pyramid grows in depth as it becomes more stable and it grows in width as it becomes more profitable. But each person employed in the pyramid is paid a wage and there is an opportunity to move up through the pyramid, though the opportunity is limited by the decreasing number of positions at each higher layer.

Understanding the dynamics of corporate structure and its culture early in a career can improve the opportunity for movement to higher layers and reduce the frustration caused by stagnation. The best opportunity for growth and success is to learn and understand the corporate structure that drives the company that employs you.

The pyramid hierarchy organization of today's corporate structure is facing some revision. Eventually the preferred corporate structure will become a network. As the cost of the tools of production increases more and more, entrepreneurs are choosing to build a company through franchising or through the use of independent contractors. Since most new jobs are created in companies of fewer than 100 people, the trend will be to contract out many tasks to independent contractors or to companies specializing in one task of a traditional corporate department. Accounting, for instance, is one department that is often performed off site by a service agency.

As more people become better educated, their choice is to offer their services through their own company. As the computer proliferates through our society, it is becoming relatively easy to conduct a service business from a remote location. FAX machines and computer modems make it possible to communicate easily anywhere that telephone lines exist. With the advent of satellites and satellite dishes, even the lack of telephone lines will not be a restriction.

Temporary employment agencies have sprung up in many fields to provide the equivalent of independent contractors to companies trying to maintain a stable core employment level. With the increase in regulations and paperwork required by both government agencies and their own internal organizations, companies are trying to reduce cost by contracting out such tasks.

More and more companies such as Amway, Mary Kaye, A.L. Williams, Avon, and others are developing corporate structures that include independent contractors as the dominant work force. The work force operates as a network with minimal ties to the corporate parent. Communications with the parent is restricted to the purchase of the product for resale.

The desire for corporations to provide more and more benefits and services to their employees has resulted in the development of a socialist culture in many large corporations. The bureaucratic restrictions become more frustrating to younger employees facing stagnation. The longer an employee stays with a pyramid corporate structure, the more difficult the choice becomes between security and stagnation or security and individuality. As benefits grow in value, they become more difficult to leave behind.

Despite the drawbacks and danger of stagnation most individuals should select a large corporation for their first job. The period from age twenty to age forty can be the most difficult to navigate in our lives and it is no different in the corporate world. Up to age twenty, many of the most important happenings are planned and coordinated by parents and teachers. Then we graduate. All lines are cut. We are told to sink or swim. We move away from school. We move away from home. The many support groups that exist in a large corporation can help ease the transition from dependent to independent. In most large corporations, clubs of all types exist for the hours away from the job. The chances of finding a group that matches your hobbies are good.

For hours spent on the job, it is important to be part of a culture in which you can feel comfortable and in which you can communicate with ease. For those coming out of school, communication is easiest if there are many others coming out of school. In a bustling, crowded workplace with many entry-level people, the experience in worker interchange, shop talk, and camaraderie is a necessary part of employee education for continued growth. Each corporate culture will have developed its own spoken language and its own body language. Becoming aware of that aspect of the culture is valuable for future communication in any environment.

For instance, communication on a one on one basis versus communication with the same people in a group meeting can be one of the more exasperating situations. The dynamics and pressures of a group meeting are much more intense and make people change behavior. It is important to understand that almost all will modify their behavior in a group situation and the many outbursts are not to be taken personally. Nevertheless, it can sometimes be disconcerting to see a friend and co-worker speak irrationally in a group session in a manner exactly opposite to his manner when speaking privately. Intimidation in group meetings creates a different role for that friend. Role playing is a large part of office politics and is usually guided by the players and their position up and down the hierarchy. You must learn to recognize role playing and distinguish between the role and the real personality. If you do not master this inconsistency forced on individuals by the pressures of the culture, you will stand alone. Learn to give and take, accept and forgive or your journey through the workplace will be a long lonely journey.

The first job selection should be made on the basis of improving and strengthening your major course of study. Promotion should not be a goal. You enter the workplace with the latest and greatest in the state of the art for your profession. You will be of most value to your new corporation technically. You will need to blend the best book experience available with sociological experience. While you may lead in technical skill, you will trail in practical specific application and in practical effective dissemination. Your first experience should be concentrated on learning how to transfer your educational skills into practical application. Office organization and politics are the domain of those experienced in this.

Working as an individual contributor allows you to spend a solid eight hours in task performance and accomplishment. Extra time can be spent taking courses required to ease transition from general education to specific tasks. The first job should last two to three years and be strictly technical task oriented. The twenties for an individual should be reserved for on-the-job training in terms of applications and organizational behavior. Most large corporations have many course offerings for further training. In some cases, the courses are provided during workday settings but most often they are presented at night after the workday.

The optimum situation for a young worker is to leave the workplace after two or three years and, with the practical experience, return to a classroom setting. In our return to the classroom, the blend of education and experience enhances our perception of the requirements and intensifies our focus into our preferred field of study. This enriched educational experience allows us to be more selective in our second entry into the workplace. In many cases, it should allow us to leapfrog several layers in the corporate bureaucracy.

If you choose the second time to open your own business, you will have the knowledge of the corporate experience to guide your dealings with large corporate clients.

Whatever direction you choose, the period of your twenties and early thirties will be the most chaotic of your career and perhaps of your life. It is the time when not only will you enter the workplace, but you also may be occupied with courting, marrying, and parenting. There will be many off-the-job distractions. It will be difficult in a balanced life to commit yourself completely to your career. It is more difficult in your twenties to choose Saturday work when the mind runs to Cape Cod or to a ski trip to your favorite mountain. An evening at work can interfere with a softball game or a night at your favorite disco. You will be unable to maximize your effort on the job. Many days will be spent just getting by as you mull over all the distractions off the job.

The early years can be the toughest on the job as well. It can be a difficult adjustment when you first realize that you are going to be working from 8 to 5 for the next forty years. For the first five years of that time you will have two weeks vacation to enjoy. This is a difficult adjustment after years in school with long summers and several vacations a year. Getting up early is never easy for a young person who loves to end the day watching a talk show host or who answers that call to a mid-week party at a favorite pub.

For all of these reasons, it is very important that you concentrate on the practical application of your technical skills. Your reputation and acceptance will grow best from this application. Help the corporate community solve those engineering problems, or those architectural problems, or those legal problems, or those accounting problems and their acceptance and love of your capabilities will be translated into acceptance and love of you as a person. Your state-of-the-art knowledge will serve you for about ten years. Prior to the end of that ten-year period, you must focus and build a reputation on a specialized portion of that knowledge. You must become recognized as an expert in a specialized field. Take courses to enhance the specialty that you choose whether it is in the same or a different field as your undergraduate degree.

The manager who hires you in any job is usually looking for good day-to-day task performance. He will not appreciate any activity from you that "rocks the boat." He is not looking for some super achievement that will propel you up the ladder. He has a job to do. He has been give routine mundane tasks to complete week after week, month after month, and he wants all his employees to help in their completion. He is not thinking of ways to propel you past him in promotions. All people at all levels want to be recognized and respected, including your boss. Your boss is looking to be promoted. Unless your boss is a rising star whose movement up the ladder is on the fast track, there will be pressures and competition between you and your boss. By concentrating on technical performance, you can dissipate those pressures. If you compete with your boss, his seniority provides him a huge advantage. As Nicholas W. Weiler says in <u>Reality and Career Planning,</u> one of the biggest myths in the corporate world is that your hard work will be recognized by your boss and he will look for ways to promote you.[1] The fact is if he knew how to advance people, he would get himself advanced. He will advance you within the group on the basis of your loyalty and technical ability to further his cause. If your boss gets promoted, you may very well get promoted if your loyalty has helped to propel him. If your boss does not get promoted and you choose to stay with that company, you must search for an opportunity outside the department, the division, or the company. Your investment in terms of seniority or vested rights is minimal at this point.

At some point in your career unless you move to a new department, division, or company, you will become stereotyped in a particular role. This is no different from an actor being stereotyped because of his role in a long-running sitcom. Stereotyping has an up-side and a down-side. The up-side is that people will become comfortable with you in a particular job setting. You will get comfortable. The down-side is it can lead to stagnation and unhappiness. It is often better to get a fresh start, a new beginning. Perhaps to fit into a particular culture, you have had to stifle your great sense of humor because your supervisor does not understand your great wit. A fresh start will allow you to free that multi-faceted character you have kept under wraps. Find someone who appreciates that great sense of humor.

Changing jobs today is more acceptable than in the past. In many cultures the diversity of experience is viewed as a plus.

As you proceed through your early thirties, your personal life will become less demanding. The thoughts of your career will become more intense. The family income needs will increase. You will have two paths from which to select. The first path will provide technical satisfaction as a principal engineer or scientist rating. The second path will provide management opportunities. Your early thirties mark a period of restlessness as you begin to search for more meaning in your life. Most likely after ten years of satisfaction from application of specific skills in your chosen field, you will want to broaden your horizons. You will want to test your skills in a supervisory role. You will want to change your success by guiding others. However, that challenge is far greater than the application of your own skills on an individual basis. Because the major corporations have become bureaucracies, rule by committee prevails. Success in guiding others requires the understanding and application of office politics. When you turn outward from a specialized view to a management view, doors closed to your initiatives will block your path unless you have done the advance work of getting approval from your peers and managers. Without prior approval, the entire process will lead to frustration and dissatisfaction. Moves can no longer be instinctive. Moves must be planned. They must be discussed one on one with anyone to be affected by the initiative. Cooperation with other managers striving to accomplish the same goal from a different department and perspective is paramount to success. Management clubs and other management support organizations usually exist to allow a manager to build deeper more meaningful relationships with peers for greater understanding.

When you begin your first supervisory role, there are two basic rules to follow:

1. Serve only one master -- when you take your first supervisory role, your desire to be accepted by the others will be strong. Your first inclination will be to serve all other supervisors equally to be on good terms with all. Beware. Be on good terms with all only to the degree that it does not detract from 100 percent satisfaction with your direct supervisor. If you reach decisions that serve others at the risk of undermining his position -- Stop! Do not dissipate your actions; this will dissipate your support. Your direct supervisor should be treated as your mentor. If your philosophy differs from that of your mentor, do not reach unilateral decisions that benefit other supervisors. Discuss the philosophy with your mentor. Act only after the two of you have reached a consensus. Just as you would do nothing to lose the support of your father, do nothing that will lose the support of your mentor. Loyalty is rewarded with loyalty.

If you cannot work within that context, change bosses. Chemistry between boss and employee is important for the cultivation of a positive frame of mind. A positive frame of mind is necessary to apply the technique of Be-Do-Have. Your boss is in a position to teach you what you need to know about the corporate culture.

2. Master the art of 3C's-Communication, Coordination, and Cooperation. These three can solve more problems than all the technical skills. People often state that the problem is communication, or coordination, or cooperation but are unable to solve it because they have not developed the skills to communicate, coordinate, or cooperate effectively. In corporate societies, these are usually considered secondary. Unfortunately, to

solve most problems, these skills are truly primary.

The following list of practices will help you to develop your 3C skills and increase your problem solving capability in the corporate culture.

1. Prepare a list of all tasks, small and large, short-term and long-term, and update each morning. This is the first rule of coordination and of communication. If you forget tasks, large and small, you are poorly organized. If you are poorly organized, you cannot coordinate and communicate properly. The confidence of others in your ability to coordinate and communicate will be eroded. When you are given a task, however minor, write it down. If someone asks that you change account #2000 from $2 to $5, write it down. If someone asks you to change the test time from 2 p.m. to 4 p.m., write it down. Cross the tasks off your list as they are completed, but keep the list as a record. A daily calendar is the best tool for this purpose.

2. Review the list first thing each morning and prioritize the tasks for the day. This will help you develop a routine for the timely completion of all tasks. People will know they can expect a timely response from you.

3. Return all telephone calls as promptly as possible. Generally, people call because they have a genuine need. Foster the practice of cooperation and communication by responding quickly.

4. Completion of each task requires employee interchange with the intention of helping those employees. Help others to do their job more easily. This is the essence of cooperation.

5. Treat everyone with courtesy. If you treat people the way you would want to be treated, people will look forward to working with you.

6. Treat everyone with respect. Most people want to do a good job. Most people believe they have something to contribute and most do. Everyone needs recognition and acceptance.

7. Listen. This is a rule taught by all communication courses from Dale Carnegie to Toastmaster Clubs.

8. Do not assume. Do not assume an employee will know or will see what you see. Communicate clearly, concisely, and thoroughly.

9. Prepare a plan for all tasks on the list. The plan may only take five minutes but it will provide a guideline from which all team members can coordinate. Always agree on at least two milestones -- the start date and the completion date.

10. Include in each plan a schedule with milestones and employee responsibility for each milestone. This helps develop all 3C's.

As you enter your mid thirties, you should have made at least one change in your career. It is a time when most people begin to question their direction in both their private lives and in their career choices. Most career changes take place after this period of self-analysis. You will begin to realize that your drive for success is a drive from within. Outside influences will become secondary. The success of outside interaction will become more of a measure of the success from the inner drive. You will become more relaxed and comfortable about who you are, but you will question the direction you have selected to satisfy that inner drive. You will begin to think about developing a better balance in your life.

At the same time, your daily routine should become more satisfying. You will be sought out for your advice. Your opinion will be respected. You will be accepted. It will be your turn to provide guidance to those less experienced. You will become the bridge between general management and individual contributors. You will interpret policy and guide the less experienced. There is a very good management technique that can assist you in guiding the younger experienced people searching for the respect and acceptance that you have gained. This technique is called the 3V's- Visibility, Visibility, and Visibility. Unlike the real estate term, location, location, and location, the 3V's do have three distinct definitions.

The first and most critical is visibility to one's supervisor. Everyone wants to contribute and be respected. If they are not allowed to contribute and they are not treated with respect, their performance will deteriorate. It is important that the supervisor review the performance of all workers and provide thanks for their contribution. This is visibility of performance. Quality circles can be valuable for allowing all workers to contribute their suggestions to the team and to receive visibility for those suggestions.

The second visibility is an understanding by the worker of how their contribution fits into the completed product. If workers are told only to consider their own task, their interest will decrease. With the acute division of labor today, tasks can become mundane unless they are presented as a necessary cog in the manufacture of the wheel. Of course the preferred practice would be to train each individual to perform each task in the manufacture of a large assembly or completion of a new design and rotate the workers regularly. At a minimum, workers must have visibility into the completed product and all its parts. They then can more readily share in the accomplishment of each completed product.

The third visibility is to provide each worker with a view of the corporate organization, goals, and performance. To build loyalty and respect for the organization, employees need visibility into the corporate family.

In summary, the Principle of Visibility provides visibility of job performance to an employee's supervisor, provides visibility of the employee's contribution with respect to the whole, and provides visibility of the employee's contribution with respect to the corporate goals.

The 3C's and the 3V's will ensure growth in your career as you develop the teamwork necessary in projects with multiple departments and many individuals. They will serve you well when you deal one-on-one with any worker.

When you reach the forties, you will either be a rising star and your career will become an expanding part of your life or you will have chosen a balance and much of your spare time will be spent contributing to causes outside your career. Either path can be very rewarding. You may also fluctuate. A long-term project may require three years of dedicated career orientation and then, perhaps, you'll spend three years coaching youth soccer or baseball. The key is not to let frustration grow. Go with the flow. If you are career oriented and choose the corporate path, just do it. If you want balance, let your supervisor know and just do it. Do not be career oriented and apologize all the way. Do not strive for balance and apologize for a day's work for a day's pay. Do not select one and expect the rewards of the other. Select and accept.

If you select balance, your boss will respect the choice. He will appreciate the loyalty and performance and dependability to complete more mundane routine tasks that free him to initiate and create.

When you are in your forties and fifties many outlets outside the workplace can provide satisfaction. Two simultaneous careers are possible as teachers, appraisers, real estate agents, insurance agents, craftsmen, coaches, and many others. Service clubs are available for raising funds and participating in worthy causes.

For most employees, the fifties is a time to enjoy the day-to-day activity, to take one day at a time. It is a time to apply the lessons of thirty years. It is time to teach and direct those in the early phase of their careers. Your knowledge and experience will become an asset to your company. Life for many becomes smoother and easier.

As more and more people retire from corporate life at age sixty or earlier, more plans are being made to continue work in a second career after corporate life.

One of the most intriguing developments in the 1980s was the personal computer. The personal computer has begun to alter the work habits of many people. People dealing in the Information Age can set up a workplace at home or in a small office. With FAX and modems, they can communicate anywhere in the world. They are never isolated, yet work at their own pace and with a balance in their life. Self-employment and independent contractors are the major trend of the 1990s. More and more people will select this option as they become versed in modern communication. More and more corporations will accept the new communications as it becomes cost effective. Many small local workplaces for the convenience of employees will begin to replace the large central locations. Plan your career to take advantage of this trend.

CHAPTER 10

LETTING THE CHILD FLOURISH

Many, as they begin this chapter, will be incredulous. Playing is utopian. How can anyone shape a life while "goofing off." As children, we all are admonished about play. Following the work ethic is how you shape your life. You do as much as you can do and then do more until you have all that you need so you can be what you want to be. The theory is that, once you reach your goal, you then can enjoy a little leisure.

Therefore our daily schedule says we work first and then we play. We work all week, then we play on the weekend. We go to school and then we play. We do our homework and then we play. The best, high-energy, most productive part of our day is reserved for work. If we do it any other way, we feel guilty.

We have progressed to some degree, however. We know that we need breaks from work to maintain our health. We need to take breaks every morning and afternoon. We need a weekend off. We need to get away for a week or two every six months. We need to clear our minds to rest, to create a diversion from our work. Play is accepted more today. But it still is considered primarily a diversion from the task at hand. Play has not been accepted as a legitimate need of our mental and physical well-being. Play has not been accepted as a basic biological need. But it is. Play is as crucial to our physical health as work is to our financial health. Play is as important to our biological production as work is to our economic production. Work satisfies the needs of society; play satisfies our social needs.

Somehow we must step back through that transparent invisible barrier that separates work and play. Somehow we must find a way to blend the two for the mutual benefit of society and the individual. When we play, we are more creative. When we play, we are more loving. When we play, we are more giving. We are more entrepreneurial when we play. We are more adventurous when we play. Many of our greatest discoveries are made while we play.

Think back to your childhood. Select a time as a child when you were happiest. Associated with that happiness you will probably find a large element of creativity, of discovery, of adventure, of pure joy. As children we learned things more easily. We picked up new ideas. We learned new subjects. We spoke more than one language. All was done naturally and matter-of-factly without much instruction or discipline. We explored. We discovered. We reveled in the discoveries.

Throughout my life I have had a strong entrepreneurial nature. I believe this was developed from the play in the first twelve or thirteen years of my life. My family moved several times during those years. Each move was seen as an opportunity to explore new territories, to make new discoveries. Two moves were most significant. The first was from the city to the country. We moved into an old farmhouse that had been converted to a duplex. One side was owned and occupied by a delightful Irish family whose parents had immigrated from Ireland. We occupied the other apartment. Our new territory for exploration was expansive. Land to explore on the house side of the road stretched back one mile to a large pond. The barn side of the road had land stretching back for over a mile, and it had a large brook meandering through its many acres. The nearest neighbor on either side was several hundred yards away.

My brothers and I would set out in the morning and spend entire days meandering over this large, exciting territory. Each day we made new discoveries. Each day our minds became aware of the possibilities of nature and the potential in ourselves. Play was never boring. There were never enough hours to play out all our fantasies or to curb our excitement for new explorations.

Then we moved two miles further into the country, and the size of our territory for exploration grew larger. Our nearest neighbor was 500 to 600 yards on either side. The seven children played and created new games, undertook new explorations, and played. We blended work and play.

Phil Donahue talks about the play of childhood and its effect on our learning and creativity. He quotes Montague:

"Play" is nature's instinctive vehicle for learning--a combination of imagination, creativity, and curiosity that is purely a creation of the neocortex: our thinking brain. In play, says Montague, we can find the roots of our adult capacities to think creatively and flexibly, to innovate, adapt, change. We are playful mammals all our lives, and that has been the reason for our remarkable adaptability and achievement as a species.[1]

The need for play continues throughout our years. We need entertainment to keep our "juices" flowing. We need exercise and sport to stay fit and to eliminate the nervous tension built up through our chores and work. We need to putter around the house to fix things that aren't broken, to play in the flower garden, to prune the trees. Some of my most creative thoughts occur when I shoot baskets for thirty to sixty minutes behind the house after supper. As I concentrate on aiming and delivering the ball, my mind is freed from all the day's concerns. New creative thoughts flow in to take their place.

Most of us work Monday through Friday and on Saturday and Sunday we look for diversion. Many go skiing in the winter and to the beaches in the summer. Many play golf each weekend. Many go hiking or camping. Others party or go dancing. Millions go to restaurants. We never stop searching for new ways to play.

When we play, we concentrate more easily. Our mind turns inward and connects to our subconscious. It provides time to fully integrate physical, mental, and spiritual. We concentrate more freely and with greater ease. There are seldom intrusions from the day's worries and cares. Time passes more quickly and easily. Our personality turns positive and loving. Our teammates, and even our competitors, become our friends. Everyone becomes focused on the same goal and we pull together. Aches and pains disappear. We express ourselves without self-consciousness or fear. We become all those things we believe we can be. We believe ourselves to be successful and contributors. We sometimes become courageous. Play helps us physically and mentally. It reduces stress and diffuses aggression. Play helps us biologically and psychologically.

When playing, we are flirting with the subconscious. Play takes us away from reality and somehow stimulates a part of our mind that generates joy, excitement, frivolity, and happiness. There are three parts to our personality. These are the ego, the superego and the id. The ego is that part of the personality that serves as the organized conscious mediator between a person and reality. It functions in a way to adapt a person's perception to reality and adjusts its personality to reality. The superego is that part of the personality that analyzes parental conscience and the rules of society. It is the bridge between ego and id between conscious and subconscious. The superego functions to punish or reward through a sense of moral attitudes, conscience, and a sense of guilt. The id, on the other hand, is completely subconscious. It is the source of psychic energy derived from instinctual needs and drives.

When we play, we are flirting with the id. We remove our thinking from the conscious reality of our daily routine and connect with the pleasures and desires of our world of fantasy. We satisfy some of the urges that we keep pent up when we must deal with reality and survival. We leave the reality behind and in a completely different part of our anatomy. The conscious part of the mind is freed to watch and relax. The conscious part of our mind becomes a spectator. Stress and anxiety are released because our concentration on that part of the cerebrum is broken. We give reality a rest. The neurons relax. Tension dissipates. The part of the brain that we use for work is rested.

Sigmund Freud developed psychoanalytic theory. "Freud compared the human mind to an iceberg. The small part that shows above the surface of the water represents conscious experience. The much larger mass below water level represents the unconscious, a storehouse of impulses, passions, and inaccessible memories that affect our thoughts and behavior."[2]

In the Introduction to Psychology, the id, ego, and superego are defined as follows:[3]

THE ID. The id is the most primitive part of the personality, from which the ego and the superego later develop. It is present in the newborn infant and consists of the basic biological impulses (or drives): the need to eat, to drink, to eliminate wastes, to avoid pain, and to gain sexual pleasure. Freud believes that aggression is also a basic biological drive. The id seeks immediate gratification of these impulses. Like a young child, the id operates on the pleasure principle: it endeavors to avoid pain and to obtain pleasure, regardless of the external circumstances.

THE EGO. Children soon learn that their impulses cannot always be gratified immediately. Hunger must wait until someone provides food. The satisfaction of relieving bladder or bowel pressure must be delayed until the bathroom is reached. Certain impulses--hitting someone or playing with the genitals--may elicit punishment from a parent. A new part of the personality, the ego, develops as the young child learns to consider the demands of reality. The ego obeys the reality principle: the gratification of impulses must be delayed until the appropriate environmental conditions are found. For example, taking the real world into consideration, the ego delays satisfaction of sexual impulses until conditions are appropriate. It is essentially the "executive" of the personality: it decides what actions are appropriate and which id impulses will be satisfied and in what manner. The ego mediates among the demands of the id, the realities of the world, and the demands of the superego.

THE SUPEREGO. The third part of the personality, the superego, is the internalized representation of the values and morals of society as taught to the child by the parents and others. It is essentially the individual's conscience. The superego judges whether an action is right or wrong. The id seeks pleasure, the ego tests reality, and the superego strives for perfection. The superego develops in response to parental rewards and punishments. It incorporates all the actions for which the child is punished or reprimanded, as well as all the actions for which the child is rewarded.

When you play, you bypass the ego and the superego. You become more childlike and carefree. You avoid the reality of the ego. You avoid the parental consciousness and the rules and regulations of society and connect with the desires of the subconscious. Play has a strong element of being. Play is a time when you feel more loving, more giving, wiser, more enthusiastic, more energetic, more adventurous.

Throughout our lifetime, we live to play. Whether play is known as dancing or chess or sex or soccer, it is our preferred state of being. It is the most natural state. Whereas we must focus ourselves to work, we seldom have to force ourselves to play. Whereas we may avoid work, we search for opportunities and ways to play. The flow from the subconscious is easy and pleasing. Play is the most natural thing in the world.

Adam and Eve were created in the Kingdom of God. They had all they needed and all they should ever want to live a life of fulfillment and contentment. Fulfillment of their sexual pleasure would procreate. Offspring would continue to be fulfilled in the same manner. Play would fill their days. Abundance filled their surroundings. They would know only one side of the personality--the id.

One parental law was put in place. They should not eat the forbidden fruit. This was the formation of the superego. By violating that one parental law, they passed through a psychological barrier. Innocence was joined by guilt. Joy was joined by despair. Courage was joined by fear. Bliss was joined by pain. Good was joined by ill. Play was joined by work. The path between the id and the superconscious was joined by a path to the superego and the ego.

By eating the forbidden fruit, they awakened the dormant superego in their personality. They felt guilt for the first time. They feared the loss of the love of God-- parental love. They perceived evil when all they had known was good. As the story unfolds, they are forced to work to exist, to work for their food. The reality of the ego was formed. Gratification had to be postponed until the realities were fulfilled. The superego had to develop rules and standards to balance the needs of the ego and the id.

Babies are born with the same one dimensional personality. Slowly the superego and the ego mature and complete the three dimensions to their personality. If the three dimensions are not nurtured and balanced, behavior grows erratic. If we satisfy only the ego, we grow weary and age prematurely. If we satisfy only the superego, we grow rigid and inflexible, and we are unable to express our feelings. If we satisfy only the id, we become undisciplined and unable to provide for ourselves. But the three together allow us to negotiate the realities of our daily lives, to function with proper restraints among the many views of society, and to create and evolve by living our fantasies.

When we have a balanced personality and the ego, superego, and id are all satisfied, we are closer to living the gospel "sow so others may reap, reap what others have sown." We are willing to operate in consort with others. We are willing to create together. We are willing to love, to give, to receive, and to share. We are willing to motivate without fear of personal loss from competitiveness.

When our personality is functioning on all three cylinders, the expression of the id allows us to share even our homes with others. In many cases when the id is the dominant part of our personality, we are able to love even those we generally do not understand. We accept. We do not judge the values of others. How many of us have gone to a picnic and found ourselves communicating with people with whom we generally find it difficult to communicate. We operate at a different level of consciousness. We share. We assist. We love. We participate and cooperate with vigor. That level is maintained until the picnic ends. Why can't we maintain the same open mind at all times?

Perhaps no society has played more or had more fun than the American society. We invent new games with enthusiasm and with ease. We try new products. We start new trends. We enjoy change. No society has created or discovered like the American society. Are the two traits of play and creativity linked? Most likely they are.

Now let's go back to the chapter on biology. In that chapter we talked about the release of hormones and chemicals from the brain that were transported through the nervous system to make the body function properly. When the proper chemicals and hormones are generated, we are completely at
ease, maybe even on a high. We see and understand things more clearly. We see things that we had missed. We feel good physically.

Some studies have shown that these chemicals and hormones are generated more effortlessly by our system when we play. When we play and eliminate most of the turbulence around us, we focus more on each action. We focus on the follow-through of a backhand in tennis. We focus on the follow-through of our hands in the golf swing. We focus all our powers of hand and eye coordination to make a basket. This total concentration increases the communication between mind and body and allows the nervous system to generate and carry-out more accurate commands for the generation of chemicals and hormones. We are communicating consciously and subconsciously to bring all our internal strength to the success of that activity. We block out everything external. We are communicating between mind and hands, mind and feet, mind and eyes.

When we are at play, the ego and superego are dismissed. We are connected to the id. As stated earlier, our most natural path is internal from the conscious, to the subconscious, to the superconscious and to everything and everyone in the universe. Others pick up our communications through this path from the universe, through the superconscious, the subconscious, and to the conscious. We are connected in a more natural way with those we play. This is a more powerful but easier path for us. During those instances of intense play, the more conscious path through the spoken word or gesture is secondary. When we connect in a more natural path, all the stresses and anxieties through the conscious verbal path are eliminated. The body does not need to generate the chemicals and hormones needed for confrontation or aggression. The body generates only the chemicals and hormones needed for understanding and love and giving.

The admonition to turn the other cheek comes from this knowledge. When we turn the other cheek, we stop the flow of chemicals and hormones needed for aggression and confrontation. When we stop this flow, we spare ourselves the psychological damage that is more harmful than the physical damage. Our progression through life in a fruitful rich manner is contingent on our ability to think straight, to keep our goal in focus, and to keep our thoughts and deeds flowing in one direction like the flow of a river. When we respond to taunts and refuse to turn the other cheek, we may gain some temporary instant gratification from physical response, but we introduce a vortex in the flow of the river, which carries turbulence for a much longer period. When we play with the proper attitude, we are able to walk away from confrontation. We play within the accepted rules. There is no psychological damage. The flow is in one direction.

In an article appearing in the May 1989 issue of Esquire magazine, "The Chemistry of Love," John Poppy describes a new field of research that was created fifteen years ago called psychoneuroimmunology (PNI). In the article psychologist Dr. Robert Ader from the University of Rochester, who founded PNI, discusses his experiment in 1974 that led him and immunologist Nicholas Cohen to PNI. Dr. Ader found that the immune system is influenced by both the nervous system and the endocrine system and presumably it is via these same channels that behavior can influence the immune system. The article points out that good feelings actually start up chemical reactions in the body that may boost the immune system -- particularly when those good feelings are directed toward other people. Other studies have shown that people who do volunteer work outlived people who did no volunteer work. Apparently doing and contributing to the well-being of others is the most powerful of all stimulants to longevity and health.

In his article, John Poppy describes the affects of neuropeptides, "The human body produces its own supplies of the chemical known as neuropeptides from cells in the brain, in other organs, and of all places, in the immune system... Neuropeptides are as potent as any drug you can take into your body from outside... They are nothing but strings of amino acids... are short strings, created in nerve cells straight off DNA."

These words appeared in the same May 1989 Esquire magazine in an article titled "The Drug Trap." "When you're living a good life, your body is exquisitely balanced, producing the right amount of specific chemical substances at the right time to arouse you, relax you, reduce pain, produce feelings of pleasure, or fortify the immune system."

Again, in the same May 1989 Esquire in an article Physiology of Sex," George Leonard comments, "Vigorous exercise increases the testosterone level in one's blood and so does sexual arousal. A moderate increase in natural testosterone is known to increase oxygen uptake, build protein, alleviate depression and strengthen the immune system. Both sex and exercise are members of the class of human activity that generally produces ew-stress -- that is good stress--rather than distress. Ew-stress releases the various peptides that make you feel good and bolster your immune system, and also reduces the long-term level of stress hormones in the bloodstream."

Something as good as play must become a regular part of our lives. When you are most tired some night and you are just sitting there thinking of your problems, get up from your chair and do something enjoyable. Start to play chess at the kitchen table or Jeopardy on your computer. Go outside for a walk. Your cares will melt away with ease. You'll find yourself suddenly counting your blessings. Dale Carnegie said it best, "Act Enthusiastic and you'll be Enthusiastic!"

You must begin to make play a regular part of your life. There must be no guilt associated with this. Integrate play into your life at two levels--first on a routine planned basis and secondly on a spontaneous basis. Make humor, joy, and laughter a regular part of your life. It breeds life enhancement.

To introduce play on a routine basis, develop a hobby. The hobby can be something you do alone but it is more enriching if you do it with others. Many people join bowling leagues, or softball leagues and enjoy either year after year. Perhaps your activity is a theater or drama club, a chess club, or a bridge club. Join a group that will provide you with the opportunity to plan for and reflect on that activity. The thoughts will raise your level of joy during more mundane periods of the week.

Secondly, become more spontaneous in your playfulness. Share jokes or witticism with your coworkers and friends. Go to a movie on the spur of the moment. Select a restaurant at the end of the work day. These actions provide a lift. We all love surprises. Surprises generate healthy biological reactions which create enthusiasm and translate to joy and happiness.

You can start right now. Call a friend and chat about some pleasant experience since you've been together last. See how the laughter makes you feel better. Get up and go for a walk. Feel the benefits physically and mentally. Plan more play in your life.

CHAPTER 11

THE MEANS FOR THE BEGINNING

Material goods ease our present burden. When income exceeds outgo, we begin to relax and to enjoy. Our spirit is high because our freedom of movement is easy. All the goods flow to us. We have funds to buy new clothes. We have funds to buy a new car. We spend on a trip to our favorite get-away spot. It's the good life. What destroys the reality of the good life is the mindset that we live in the midst of scarcity, that there is not enough to go around, that the earth's resources will dry up and we will expire as a species.

We in fact live in great abundance. There is more than enough for everyone and we must unlock the doors, find the keys, open the door to let the abundance flow. Everyone can do this for themselves because everyone has a direct line to GOD. He is the source of our abundance.

Material is about the abundance that is within all of us. The easiest way for us to shape our life through Material is to change our perception of material. The current perception is that it is difficult to generate, that there is a limited amount of it, that only a few can obtain it, and that it is an end in itself.

These perceptions were formed from a contradiction in terms of our spiritual and physical teachings. This contradiction in terms has set up a conflict in ourselves, which disrupts the flow within us. The conflict has created a vortex in our spiritual, mental, and physical system that disrupts our flow of energy. This disruption slows or even stops the flow of abundance which comes from that energy.

This faulty perception may have started with the first two human beings, Adam and Eve. When they were created by God, they had all that they needed to enjoy life to the fullest. They would populate the earth and share all their gifts with their offspring. The enlightenment, the generosity, and the innocence flowing from this abundant life style would create a population of happy content people willing to contribute to the awareness of all others.

But that perception of abundance was colored by the actions of Adam and Eve, and man began to take twists and turns in his evolution which led him away from that perception. The primary shift in perception was that abundance came from outside man and only if he cultivated the land. Adam and Eve went from a life style of ease and abundance to a life style of hard work.

We have all been exposed to such a change in perception. The most common change in perception usually occurs through the use of alcohol. Reality returns once the effects of alcohol recede. How many would continue the alcohol-induced perception if it were not for the debilitating degenerating affect of alcohol on our health and on our performance? Alcohol frees us of the perception of limitation. But it is artificially induced and destructive. Each person's goal should be to shape life through a natural change in perception. The goal can be achieved by eliminating the vortex and recovering the initial perception shared by Adam and Eve. We must learn to go with the flow, to go with our inner feelings and intuition.

Materialism has become a contradiction in our society. Instinctively we strive for more. We are encouraged to consume more to keep our lines of production flowing. Yet, we are told of the scarcity of our resources. Consume but beware of limitations. We are urged to compete and consume our fair share before it is all consumed by others. We are like a group of twenty children given a five gallon jar of ice cream to share. Our drive is instinctive, but we are filled with some guilt.

At its worst, material becomes a controlling influence in our lives. At its most supportive, material provides us with the physical goods and leisure time that allow us to increase awareness and foster change, which leads to personal growth. At its best it blends with contribution to increase awareness, foster change and lead to the growth and enlightenment of others.

Material possessions are not an end in themselves. Material possessions are only the beginning. Material possessions are the fuel that propels us along our journey, along our destiny. Without sufficient fuel, life is a struggle for survival. Without the fuel we cannot shape our lives eleven other ways. When we become preoccupied with survival, we are without the time or desire to search for a higher self.

When all our energy is required to provide the basics of food and shelter, we have little desire for self-improvement. Too often, however, when we do succeed in acquiring wealth in excess of our needs, the material becomes an end in itself.

The current perception is that material is difficult to generate and requires hard work. That those fortunate to have the tools of production obtain it and enjoy it in abundance. Once obtained it should be enjoyed for its creature comforts. This is Doing and then Being.

We all have a direct line to God and the Universal Mind. There should be no false gods interrupting that direct line to God. False gods in our society can be any number of people who try to influence us, and who would manipulate us. These are all outside influences that interrupt the flow within us and our direct line to the Universal Mind. All communications with other people, all other connections other than through the direct line are secondary communication lines. All other communications are reactions to our direct desires and actions.

If we communicate through the direct line to the Universal Mind, then all responses to our wishes flow through us and at times come through in the form of suggestions, recommendations, and gifts from supervisors, friends and relatives.

Our understanding of the direct line provides an alternate perception which proceeds along the following path to abundance. Material is easy to generate. It requires that we accept the flow of abundance from within, that there are no limitations except those created by man. Once material is obtained it should be used in some part to contribute to the enlightenment of others. This is Being and then Doing.

Doing before Being makes us work as hard as we can to accumulate, to build security so that we may then have the time and the means to be what we want to be. This requires using our competitive instinct and our manipulative skills to win a large share of very limited resources.

Being before Doing means involving the conscious to subconscious path of our mind in finding the answers intuitively. We must Be before we Do. By Being before

Doing we "go with the flow." We trust in the river and let it carry us along. Doing becomes a mere matter of directing our course around bends, rocks, and hanging branches.

Limitation, scarcity, difficulty in generation --these are a part of our perception which we address with supervisors, friends, and relatives. These are manipulations. The perception masks the true order of nature -- the world has tremendous abundance and whenever man has searched he has found all the resources necessary to propel him along his path of greater awareness, change, and growth. It is always revealed when we take the direct path within.

When we come to believe that the natural order of things is abundance, sharing, and the enlightenment of others, our instincts, inner drive, and consumption are in harmony. The vortex of instinctive drive for abundance and limitation is eliminated. The flow of energy within us increases. The natural order is that by looking within, man will always discover the resources needed. There is no limitation, there is only a perception masking the abundance. Automobiles were always possible. Their need was not perceived. Oil has been available, but its use was not perceived. Abundance is the natural order. We need only perceive, discover, and receive.

When we begin to think in terms of abundance and refuse to accept limitation, we will find the need for competition dissolve. Competition is for those who perceive limitation, who act for survival. When Adam and Eve perceived abundance, their every need was filled without toil. When they perceived guilt and limitation, they had to work just to survive. Remember their surroundings did not change. The abundance surrounded them, but their perceptions changed, and their flow of abundance from within was blocked. Our own perceptions block the flow within us. Our own lack of awareness limits our energy and wisdom.

To energize the flow we need to change our sequence for acquiring from Doing to Having to Being to a sequence of Being to Doing to Having. By Doing first we are using only conscious communication with others to drive our growth. By Being first we use our instinctive subconscious drive which eases the flow of communication with others. When we do first, we do not have the intuitive inner drive tied to the doing. The doing is without the proper inspiration. It is without moral context. There is no joy in the doing. Too often we are doing something that will let us be something at a later date, perhaps after retirement.

When you do something with inspiration, it is because that something is flowing from within. It is not an action triggered only by a command or request from another person. Try Being. Consider one thing that you desire strongly. Focus on its manifestation by bringing it to mind daily. The means to acquire that thing will be revealed intuitively. Do the things that flow from intuition. Call the people who come to mind. Write down those plans that enter your mind. Complete each task as it surfaces in your mind. Do not reveal your desire to others. If that desire is right for you, you believe it is right for you, and you accept its manifestation, it will be fulfilled.

The key to its manifestation is its flow from within as you flow out through communication with other people.

Dr. Robert Anthony calls this the law of circulation. He describes his law of circulation in this way:

"A good example is a pond. If water only comes into the pond, soon the pond will stagnate and will no longer support life. Now, if water only goes out of the pond, the pond will soon dry up and no longer be able to support life. We can take our cues from the examples of nature; it is the same in our financial lives. As we circulate our money freely, more money flows into our lives."[1]

One of the best uses of our material wealth is in the increase of our awareness of the other eleven functions that balance our life. By spending wisely we can improve our knowledge, improve our diet, and improve our mental and physical health. The higher levels of awareness we reach the more we improve the flow in and out of our life. The flow for material should be from abundance to awareness to change to growth to contribution. The list of goods and services that will strengthen that flow is endless.

Every individual aspires to something greater or desires respect for current achievements. The blockages of inspiration and respect are limitations self-imposed by perceptions or imposed by the misperceptions of others. Begin to understand and remove the blockages and awareness, and change and growth will lead to respect and dignity. No person who has amassed a great fortune ever did so by trying to maintain the status quo.

All fortunes were the result of new products or services fueled by an increase in awareness, which lead to an idea for change and growth. All improvements in our life, all increases in our standard of living were fueled by intuitive drive first, which led to Doing second.

We can shape our life by rethinking our perceptions of material goods. We can shape our life by perceiving material as a flow of abundance from within that leads to an increase of awareness, change and growth within us and an acceptance of our responsibility for the enlightenment and love of our neighbor. When we see the abundance flow from within, all competition turns to cooperation and contribution.

CHAPTER 12

RELEASING MYTHS, PHOBIAS, AND GUILT

How free we become depends in large measure on how attentive we are in balancing the other components in our lives. It is relatively easy to free ourselves of external commitments and responsibilities. It is relatively easy to commit ourselves to some task that will bring freedom in our surroundings. But, to truly be free we must free ourselves from the false values, myths, fears, guilts, and phobias that hinder us from within.

Freedom must be built from inside out. We must start by building a stable vibrant internal environment based on high self-esteem. It takes some part of all previous components to develop that strong internal environment. How free can we be if poor nutritional habits leave us without energy to function? How free can we be if our work and play routine provides only boredom? How free can we be if, in this society, we cannot read and write?

Freedom is not something that we can proclaim or invent. Laws and regulations can only set the parameters and boundaries of freedom. How each person functions within those parameters and boundaries depends on the internal degree of freedom whatever people or governments proclaim.

Freedom is unique for every individual. Freedom consists of two parts, Freedom of Being and Freedom of Doing.[1] Freedom of Being springs from the knowledge and awareness that stimulates the thought process. Freedom of Doing are the activities that spring from that thought process. Freedom is a composite of our thoughts and actions. We are free when we can be who we are and when we can do what we really want to do. We are free when we can be true to our values without judging the values of others. A scenario of an individual acting with freedom reveals a person with high self-esteem, total self-confidence, high in energy, filled with love, true to personal values, and willing to contribute to the well-being of others.

Freedom has a very aggressive nature when we examine it on the surface. Many people have died to defend their freedom. Freedom is as basic as the need to eat and to drink. And to deny freedom to an individual can raise a wrath seldom seen when the person is denied food or drink.

Freedom is difficult to define, however, because it is many different things to many different people. It is considered each person's right to be free, with each person having great latitude in expressing freedom.

Freedom should be limited only to the degree that it infringes on the safety and on the security and the freedom of movement of others. That is the role that we have defined for our town, state, and federal governments.

They are charged with providing liberty and maintaining safety and security. They maintain boundaries between countries with differing cultures and differing political systems. They maintain freedom of speech and freedom of the press. They regulate so that one may not infringe on the values of another. They create zoning so that the majority may live and work in peace and harmony. They maintain a core set of values that provide liberty with stability and security in each society. From that liberty, stability and security, individuals are free to define and live their own unique perception of freedom. Freedom is truly unique for each individual.

As in the components of biology and environment, we must add a new dimension to our thoughts of freedom. Freedom comes from deep within us. It is like an ice skater gliding over a clear thick patch of ice while pondering the reflection in the ice below. A graceful relaxed image helps the skater glide with ease and confidence. A shaky clumsy image makes the skater move uneasily and with concern.

What it takes to make one person feel free is different from what it takes for another person to feel free. One person feels free when living in the countryside amid nature. Another person can feel isolated and live in fear in the same countryside. One person living in the city feels free because of the movement of many others. Another person is intimidated and uneasy by the conflicting activity of so many in the same city. Why is it that some people feel free when self-employed and some feel free only when they can forget the job at five o'clock? Why is it that some feel free when they are alone and others feel free only when socializing? We all have a unique sense of space and isolation.

To shape our lives through freedom we must begin by examining facets of our life while listing those traits or characteristics that stop us from being who we want to be. These traits and characteristics restrict us internally and externally. External restrictions can be dealt with more easily through negotiations and discussions with those involved. Internal restrictions are negotiated with ourselves by using techniques such as creative visualizations and in discussions with family, friends, and therapists. Psychologists use techniques to change the emphasis of the conscious and subconscious mind from a negative to a positive. The techniques reach down to our basic environment, the cell, and begin the process of change and growth at that level until all levels that form our internal environment are in harmony with who we are and with what we want to do.

Listed below are some of the traits that stop us from being who we are and what we want to be:

fear of flying	poor communication
fear of public speaking	low energy level
smoking	high anxiety
weight problem	lack of enthusiasm
insecurity	selfishness
fear of socializing	lack of love for others
fear of making decisions	fear of strangers
fear of dark	fear of open or closed spaces

The list can be expanded to include many more blockages to our freedom.

These all enter our thought process to some degree and imprint negative perceptions and views on our mind that rob us of freedom of movement and action. They impact freedom of being by creating blockages in our nervous system neurons. They inhibit the flow of positive ideas from the conscious to the subconscious mind and create a self-image with lowered confidence and esteem. These blockages by inhibiting our freedom of being are then translated into inhibitions in our freedom of doing.

Our movement and actions are restricted by the false values, myths, fears, guilts, and phobias. They act as blockages in our minds. We are unable to attend a party because we have a phobia about crowds. We are unable to attend a meeting for fear we will be called on to speak. We are unable to make a decision because we have to live with the consequences. To expand our freedom of doing we must begin with our freedom of being.

To begin transforming and eliminating those fears and phobias we can select one that seems least foreboding. If it is an external boundary on our freedom, we can discuss it openly with family, relatives, and friends. We must try to build an understanding and an awareness of its negative influence. If the boundary does not impact the safety, security, and well-being of others it should be eliminated. If it does affect others, we must accept the boundary. If it is internal and private, we must begin to use a technique such as creative visualization to transform it to a positive. We must tear down the barriers and blockages in our mind. We must begin to realize that it is not reality. The understanding takes time. But with consistency and persistence, it can be eliminated from our subconscious as a negative part of our image. In the same way we can begin to eliminate false values, myths, fears, guilts, and phobias. We can transform each until we begin to recite from the following list:

I love to fly.	I am a good communicator.
I love to speak in public.	I am a non-smoker.
I am totally relaxed.	I am in control of my emotions
I am totally secure.	I love to go to parties.
I am a loving person.	I am decisive.
I love to meet new people	I love who I am.
I am fully confident.	I am full of energy.
I am enthusiastic.	I am courageous.

We can turn each negative into a positive. We can work on two or three or four or more at a time. We can increase our self-confidence and self-esteem. This will provide us with more freedom than we ever thought possible.

In his book, Phobia: The Facts Donald W. Goodwin discusses Wolpe's approach to eliminating phobias.[2] Using this approach, therapists instruct their patients to imagine or visualize their worst fears in the mildest form. When the patient's anxiety is reduced, the patient proceeds to a form of the phobia which produces a higher level of anxiety. With each level a pleasant experience is included to counteract the fear. In this way a patient's subconscious begins to look for ways to replace the negative image with a positive image.

Using another approach called cognitive therapy, psychiatrists use visualization as the key to treatment.

Donald Goodwin states, "A branch of behavior therapy called 'cognitive therapy' holds that thoughts cause feelings as well as feelings cause thoughts (a 'cognition' is a fancy word for a thought). Cognitive therapists teach their patients to substitute positive thoughts for negative thoughts. The patent for this approach no doubt belongs to Norman Vincent Peale, but cognitive therapists have approached positive thinking more systematically than Dr. Peale, and have even done studies, sometimes showing that their treatment works.

As applied to phobias, the treatment consists of training in 'self-statements.' Because people are always talking to themselves (cognitive therapy rests on this premise), why not train people to say things to themselves which make them feel better and improve their life adjustment?"[3]

Most people have had their perceptions changed by outside forces that made them implant images of fear and limitations on their subconscious. We can alter those perceptions. We can replace negative thoughts and images with positive thoughts and images.

Positive thoughts build on positive thoughts until more powerful positive thoughts enter our mind. When these are repeated, they lead to more positive thoughts. Our positive thoughts remove boundaries and blockages from our mind. Our sense of freedom grows as our confidence and self-esteem grows. We traverse roads and byways once thought inaccessible.

As we rid ourselves of myths, fears, guilts, and phobias, our values are allowed to surface. We express our values more easily with conviction. Rollo May calls freedom the mother of all values. He says, "Take the value of love. How can I prize a person's love if I know the love is not given with some degree of freedom? What is to keep this so-called love from being merely an act of dependency or conformity? For love can take concrete shape only in freedom."[4]

Rollo May calls freedom more than a value itself. He says it underlies the possibility of valuing, that it is basic to our capacity to value.

Values are personal. Each person must be free to live according to personal values if they do not affect the safety, security, or well-being of others.

Begin examining some facet of your life. What are the myths, fears, guilts, and phobias that are holding you back? Are you free to do what you want to do? Are you free to fly off to an island or are you one of millions grounded by fear of flying? Are you free to move to your special place or do your roots tie you to a place that is uncomfortable?

If you could free your own personal life from the psychological and physical bonds that keep you in the same rut week after week, it would far surpass any gain in freedom that your government can provide.

Do not look outwardly. Look inwardly. Do not look to government or to leaders. You have a unique set of values, myths, fears, guilts, and phobias. Only you have the set developed by your genetic biological self, shaped by your particular environment and nurtured by your educational background. Freedom to you is unique. It is time to Free yourself. It is time to attain the maximum growth possible with the maximum peace of mind, sense of accomplishment and well-being. Put the other eleven components to work to increase your sense of freedom.

CHAPTER 13

THE MEANS TO THE END

When we get results, we want to sustain them and we want to share them with other people. At that stage, we are prepared to move to the highest good of all concerned. We are able to take full responsibility to create a happy and abundant world for all. We then realize that materialism is not an end in itself but it is only the beginning. Materialism allows us to practice Contribution.

Contribution allows us to raise our spirit and the spirit of others. We practice it in many ways each day. We practice it when we say, "Good morning" and when we say, "Have a good day." We practice it when we tell our child the drawing is lovely. We practice it when we help our neighbors start their frozen automobile engine. All of these are sharing, giving things. We consider them as little things but they do lift the human spirit. The negative or reverse of such positive exchanges can be devastating. What if we tell our children that their drawings are not very good? What if we refuse to assist a neighbor in time of need? The accumulation of negative acts can cause much turbulence within us. It harms us and ages us and makes us stoop.

Contribution has the power to build us and rejuvenate us. It is the ability to love ourselves to such an extent that we can love who we are completely and unequivocally. It means we have the self-image and self-esteem to deal with all people as we should. We are able to communicate without rancor or hate. We are able to commit to a happy abundant world for all.

Contribution creates a closed loop between our striving and our achieving. It forms the last sector of the circle around the twelve components.

If material acquisition is the fuel needed to shape our life eleven other ways, contribution is the fuel that allows us to help others shape their lives. It is the second greatest commandment -- Love thy neighbor. It is the creation of the Kingdom of God day in and day out.

The Kingdom of God is not something out in the distance in some other galaxy. The Kingdom of God is not something in the future that will be created. The Kingdom of God is all around us and we are all creating it each day. How much each individual assists in its creation will be the measure of his contribution.

Contribution is a creative act, a positive act for the enlightenment of ourselves and our neighbors.

Contribution has many levels. In the end our growth is measured by our self-esteem. How much of ourselves do we really love and are we truly able to love our neighbors as ourselves? One barometer of growth is the degree that we retain hate, anger, envy, competition, and comparison. If we have high self-esteem, these will disappear from our emotions. If we have high self-esteem, we realize that we are the creators of our world and of our life. What we desire, what we do, and what we feel form the mental images that drive our growth. By contributing to a set of positive images we raise our awareness and the awareness of others. Confidence, self-image increases in all.

Contribution can be practiced on many levels. The easiest is a smile, a hug, and a handshake. At another level it is speaking a kind word, giving a compliment, suggesting rather than commanding, showing respect. A simple smile, hug, or a handshake from a confident self-assured friend raises the spirit. It says you're okay. It's a simple act which raises confidence and alters awareness.

Contribution can be practiced through teaching, coaching, volunteering, and donation. Contribution can be practiced through time, things, or money.

The best example of the art of contribution is through the examination of parent and child relationships. Parents contribute much time, many things, and much money to raise their own children to a level of awareness that will make them self-sufficient, confident, and contributors to their own children. This contribution by parents is conveyed usually without much thought of personal gain, but with great delight. The contribution is usually made over many years. The exchange of love between parent and child is a source of joy. Parents contribute so their children may reach new heights, pass through new boundaries, make new discoveries, and become a new source of energy to help others climb.

Parenthood is instinctive contribution. In learning to contribute, we should analyze the dynamics that drive parent-child relationships and transfer those dynamics to those outside the family. Why is love of neighbor too often so difficult? Why doesn't contribution outside the family provide the same joy as that within the family? Perhaps the negative emotions block the flow. Perhaps envy, hate, fear created by competition, and comparison block the flow.

Responsibility for enlightenment and contribution to others are recognition of the spiritual path within us. When we can transfer the same love created in a parent-child relationship, we recognize that not only parent and child are from the same bond but that all of us are from the same Universal Mind, the same Infinite Intelligence and Energy.

When an individual transfers energy from manipulation to contribution, that person acknowledges the need to love.

Shakti Gawain states it this way, "This is the process known as enlightenment, and I believe that it is an ongoing evolution of every individual which cannot be complete until all our fellow beings are sharing in it. So we are equally responsible for our own enlightenment and the enlightenment of all fellow beings on our planet."[1]

The reason for any difficulty in transferring the art of contribution from our children to our neighbor is our perception of limitation and scarcity. The view of limitation and scarcity breeds competition and comparison. It is difficult to contribute when we are trying to battle limitation and scarcity.

There are three states of existence regarding wealth. There is poverty and acceptance of poverty. There is a view of limitation and scarcity requiring a battle to obtain no less than our fair share. And finally, there is a view of abundance. Any person can select any state and pursue that state. By far the most difficult and challenging is the view of limitation and scarcity. For those who accept poverty, there is no struggle on the physical level. They are not aware of the flow from the physical to the spiritual and back but rather accept each as separate and are satisfied that each will be fulfilled in the proper time. Those who perceive limitation and scarcity but manipulate others to get a majority share are the most dangerous to themselves and to others. They are not aware of the flow from physical to spiritual and back but operate strictly on the physical level to obtain an abundance at the expense of others. The third group, a minority at this time, recognize that humans have always discovered ways as needed to provide all that is needed and that there is no end to this flow. This group accepts abundance as the natural order of things. They do not struggle for an unfair share, but they are aware that there is more than enough for everyone.

The first group and the third group believe that contribution is an extension of their existence. Both groups reject competition and comparison. Both groups accept their existence on the physical plane. One expects eventual fulfillment on the spiritual plane. The other is currently fulfilled on the spiritual plane. Those currently fulfilled on the spiritual plane understand the abundance that flows within them. The abundance flows through them in the force of creative energy. The energy is transformed to the physical realm through an idea, invention, or discovery.

The three groups work in society with their own perception of material possessions. Members of the first accept their lot on the physical plane for better or for worse, believing their reward will come at another time. The second labor for at least their fair share of the limited resources and manipulate and compete to win that share. Members of the third group accept the flow of abundance as the natural order of their lives.

To maintain that flow of abundance they realize that contribution is required. The contribution is thought of as seed. One such principle for contributing to the churches is called tithing.

But contribution is not measured in dollars and cents only. There are many facets to contribution. Many have an abundant flow of love in their lives because they contribute love to many. Many have an abundant flow of wisdom because they contribute guidance to many. Many have an abundant flow of energy and enthusiasm because they work ceaselessly and joyfully to care for those less fortunate. Many have an abundant flow of ideas because they contemplate building new goods and providing new services.

Some positions are more directly connected to contribution. Educators, trainers, coaches, clergy, doctors, nurses, social workers in many cases accepted their profession for what they could contribute rather than to obtain their fair share.

For most the art of contribution improves as we mature and grow in wisdom. As the gratification from material manifestation levels off, our search for more meaningful life increases. Do not be discouraged if contribution is not in your heart early in life. Many do not develop the art until we have learned from experiences in our life. Most of us grow up with comparison and competition and try to emulate the more successful practitioners in our midst. As we grow in maturity and self-esteem, we begin to understand and realize our uniqueness, our own individual merit with the same direct line to the Infinite Intelligence of the Universal God. We realize that we have a direct line to the source of all energy and power and that each of us has an equal opportunity to share that source. It draws us away from comparison and competition and leads us to contribution. It provides a boost at a stage in our lives when we begin to question the very need to continue. It becomes the most valid time for us to turn the flow from within to the awareness and enlightenment of others.

Most of us received many blessings as children and through early adulthood to the point of starting a family of our own. It is at that time that contribution is most apt to begin to stir in our heart and mind. In most lives, seeing the ultimate blessing, a newborn in our home, does more to stir contribution than any act up to that time. At the precious time we usually commit ourselves to the enlightenment and awareness of our own children. As their needs diminish and our drive for comparison and competition weakens, we are able to pass commitment from our children to our neighbor. As we grow, mature, improve our confidence and esteem, we become capable of manifesting love of neighbor. At that point we have truly graduated to a single most important purpose in our life.

CHAPTER 14

BUILDING OUR ROAD

Natural laws define the natural order of things. The closer we come to realizing and understanding the natural laws, the greater the flow of universal energy through us. The closer we come to the natural order in our physical, intellectual, and spiritual thoughts and actions, the more prosperity, joy, and well-being flow through us. These laws of nature are similar to the natural law of gravity. We realize the effect of gravity on our movement and build an understanding of how to function. We increase our mobility. There are many natural laws that define truth, love, faith, abundance, freedom, intuition, wisdom, and unity. As we build knowledge and awareness, we learn to modify our behavior to be in harmony with natural laws.

We have the knowledge to start reshaping our lives. We must become more aware of the flow from conscious to subconscious. Once we achieve some success in shaping our life, our energy increases. The increase in energy spurs us to continue to search and grow.

Start with a simple discussion of who you are and what you want to do. Let the answers flow smoothly and naturally from within. Be patient. Take some time. Let the answers surface. They will. As you begin to lock on the answers, you will begin to develop a sense of destiny. The path of your journey will become clearer. Your confidence will increase. Your self-esteem will grow. Get a fresh start. Begin again. Put Being before Doing. Replace competition, comparison, and manipulation with love, truth, and contribution.

BIBLIOGRAPHY

Anthony, Robert. <u>Dr. Robert Anthony's Advanced Formula for Total Success.</u> New York: Berkley Books, 1988/

Anthony, Robert. <u>Dr. Robert Anthony's Ultimate Secrets of Total Self-Confidence.</u> New York: Berkley Books, 1984.

Atkinson, Rita L.; Atkinson, Richard C.; Smith, Edward E.; Hilgard, Ernest R. <u>Introduction to Psychology.</u> Orlando, Fla.: Harcourt Brace Jovanovich, 1987.

Blumenthal, Dale. "A Simple Guide to Complex Carbohydrates." Washington, D.C.: Department of Health and Human Services, FDA Consumer Magazine, 1989.

Brown, Barbara B. <u>New Mind, New Body.</u> New York: Harper & Row, 1974.

Coleman, Richard M. <u>Wide Awake at 3:00 A.M. By Choice or By Chance.</u> New York: W.H. Freeman & Co., 1986.

Cooper, Kenneth, H. <u>Aerobics.</u> New York: M. Evans, 1968.

Dewey, John. <u>The Human Animal.</u> New York: The McMillan Company, 1916.

Donahue, Phil. <u>The Human Animal.</u> New York: Simon & Schuster, 1986.

Fromm, Erich. <u>To Have or to Be?</u> New York: Harper & Row, 1976.

Gawain, Shakti. <u>Creative Visualization.</u> New York: Bantam Books, 1985.

Gebhardt, Susan E. Nutritive Value of Foods. Washington, D.C.: U.S. Dept. of Agriculture, 1988.

Goodwin, Donald W. Phobia: The Facts. Oxford: Oxford University Press, 1983.

Hales, Dianne. The Complete Book of Sleep, How Your Nights Affect Your Days. Reading, Mass: Addison-Wesley Pub. Co., 1981.

Hill, Napoleon. Think and Grow Rich. New York. Fawcett Crest, 1960.

Jacob Stanley W.; Francone, Clarice A.; Lossow, Walter J. Structure and Function in Man.
Philadelphia: W.B. Saunders Co., 1978.

Katahn, Martin.   The 200 Calorie Solution: How to Burn an Extra 200 Calories a Day and Stop Dieting. New York: Norton, 1982.

Konishi, Frank; Kesselman, Judy R.; Peterson, Franklynn. Eat Anything Exercise Diet: How to be Slim and Fit for Life. New York: Morrow, 1979.

Leonard, George. "The Physiology of Sex." New York: Esquire Magazine, May 1989.

Levinson, Harold N. Phobia Free. New York: M. Evans & Co., 1986.

Mandino, Og. The Greatest Miracle in the World. New York: Frederick Fell, 1975.

Mawran, Frank. "Now, Hits Just Keep on Coming." Boston Glove: April 23, 1990.

May, Rollo. Freedom and Destiny: New York: Norton, 1981.

Poppy, John. "The Chemistry of Love." New York: Esquire Magazine, May 1989.

Robertson, Donald. "How 8 Glasses a Day Keep Fat Away." Los Angeles: McCall's Magazine, January 1986.

Weiler, Nicholas W. Realty and Career Planning. Reading, Mass: Addison-Wesley Pub. Co., 1989.

Calories & Weight. the USDA Pocket Guide. Washington, D.C.: U.S. Department of Agriculture, 1990.

"Cut Your Cholesterol 30 Points in 30 Days. Emmanus, Penn.: Prevention Magazine, February 1989.

Dietary Guidelines for Americans. Washington, D.C.: U.S. Dept. of Agriculture, 1990.

"The Drug Trap." New York: Esquire Magazine, May 1989.

The Living Bible. Wheaton, ILL.: Tyndale House Publishers, Inc., 1971.

The Bible, New American Version. New York: Catholic Book Publishing Co., 1970.

FOOT NOTES

Chapter 1

[1](New York: Frederick Fell), 1975, p. 99.

[2] Based on Think and Grow Rich by Napoleon Hill (New York, Fawcett Crest, 1960).

[3] Based on Dr. Robert Anthony's Advanced Formula for Total Success by Dr. Robert Anthony (New York: Berkley Books, 1988).

[4] (New York: Harper & Row, 1976), p. 109.

Chapter 2

[1] (New York: Harper & Row, 1974), p. 49.

[2] Material in Chapter 2 is based on Structure and Function in Man by Stanley W. Jacob, Clarice A. Francone, Walter J. Lossow (Philadelphia: W.B. Saunders Co., 1978).

Chapter 3

[1] Structure and Function in Man, Stanley W. Jacob, Claire A. Francone, Walter J. Lossow, PhD.; Philadelphia, Penn. W.B. Saunders Co., 1978) p. 5.

Chapter 4

[1] Shakti Gawain, Creative Visualization (New York: Bantam Books, 1985).

Chapter 5

[1] Rounded from 2955 calories per pound as shown in <u>Eat Anything Exercise Diet, How to be Slim and Fit for Life</u>. Frank Konishi, Judy Kesselman, Franklynn Peterson (New York: Morrow, 1979), Table 2-3, p. 34.

[2] "Cut Your Cholesterol 30 Points in 30 Days" (Emmanus, Penn: Prevention Magazine, February 1989), p. 37.

[3] Dale Blumenthal, "A Simple Guide to Complex Carbohydrates" (Washington, D.C. FDA Consumer Magazine, Dept. of Health and Human Services, 1989.)

Chapter 6

[1] Based on <u>Eat Anything Exercise Diet</u>: How to be Slim and Fit for Life; Frank Konishi, Judy Kesselman, Franklynn Peterson (New York: Morrow, 1979).

[2] (New York: M. Evans, 1968), p. 39.

Chapter 7

[1] <u>Dr. Robert Anthony's The Ultimate Secrets of Total Self-Confidence</u> (New York: Berkley Books, 1984), p. 46

[2] (New York: The McMillan Company, 1916), p. 62.

Chapter 8

[1] (New York: Simon & Schuster, 1985), p. 350.

[2] <u>The Complete Book of Sleep, How Your Night Affects Your Days</u> (Reading, Mass: Addison-Wesley, 1981), p. 155.

[3] <u>Wide Awake at 3:00 A.M. by Choice or by Chance</u> (New York: W.H. Freeman & Co., 1986), p. 8.

[4] <u>The Complete Book of Sleep, How Your Nights Affect Your Days</u>, p. 78.

[5] Wide Awake at 3:00 A.M., by Choice or by Chance.

Chapter 9

[1] (Reading, Mass: Addison-Wesley, 1989), p. 12.

Chapter 10

[1] The Human Animal (New York: Simon & Schuster, 1985), p. 270.

[2] Introduction to Psychology, R.L. Atkinson; E.R. Smith; E.R. Hilgard (Orlando, FL: Harcourt Brace Jovanovich, 1987), Ninth Edition, p. 429.

[3] Introduction to Psychology, p. 429.

Chapter 11

[1] Dr. Robert Anthony's Advanced Formula for Total Success (New York: Berkley Books, 1988), p. 113.

Chapter 12

[1] Rollo May, Freedom and Destiny (New York: Norton; 1981), p. 53.

[2] (Oxford: Oxford University Press, 1983), p. 106.

[3] Phobia: The Facts, p. 113.

[4] Freedom and Destiny, p. 6.

Chapter 13

[1] Creative Visualization (New York: Bantam Books, 1985), p. 28.